GRAINS AS MAINS

Laura Agar Wilson

LONDON, NEW YORK, MELBOURNE, MUNICH, AND DELHI

Senior Editor Vanessa Daubney
Senior Art Editor Sara Robin
Managing Editor Dawn Henderson
Managing Art Editor Christine Keilty
Jacket Art Editor Kathryn Wilding
Pre-Production Producer Rebecca Fallowfield
Senior Producer Jen Scothern
Art Director Peter Luff
Publisher Peggy Vance

DK INDIA
Editor Neha Ruth Samuel
Senior Art Editor Ira Sharma
Art Editor Neha Wahi
Assistant Art Editor Pallavi Kapur
Managing Editor Alicia Ingty
Managing Art Editor Navidita Thapa
Pre-Production Manager Sunil Sharma
DTP Designers Rajdeep Singh, Manish Upreti, Satish Chandra Gaur

Published in Great Britain in 2015 by
Dorling Kindersley Limited
80 Strand, London, WC2R ORL

2 4 6 8 10 9 7 5 3
001 – 271731 – Mar/2015

Copyright © 2015
Dorling Kindersley Limited
A Penguin Random House Company

A CIP catalogue record for this book is available from the British Library

ISBN 978-0-2411-8537-7

Colour reproduction by Altaimage LTD

Printed and bound in Hung Hing

Discover more at **www.dk.com**

CONTENTS

FOREWORD

As more of us have become health-conscious foodies, ancient grains have been making a comeback. Take a look at any health-food shop or wholefood section of the supermarket and you will see how popular they are.

The grains and seeds featured in this book are known as "ancient grains" because they are virtually the same now as they were when they were grown and eaten by some of the world's oldest civilizations. Now widely available, they don't just taste good; they are also highly nutritious because they really are whole grains and provide us with fibre, protein, healthy fats, vitamins, and minerals. Plus, many of these grains, such as amaranth, quinoa, and teff, are gluten-free. They originate from all over the globe, and as a great source of protein, they are ideal for vegetarians and vegans alike, but they can also enhance the health benefits of any dish that includes animal protein.

With a wide range of exciting flavours and textures, these grains can be cooked and eaten in a variety of ways. No longer should they be regarded as simply a side dish. The recipes in *Grains as Mains* set ancient grains at centre stage, demonstrating how versatile they are and how you can use them to invigorate classic dishes. You will find a wealth of useful information in the introductory chapter of this book, plus a wonderful array of exciting recipes to try – from breakfast dishes to soups, stir-fries, casseroles, and even tempting desserts.

It is my hope that, from these recipes, you will go on to experiment with grains in new dishes yourself.

As a self-confessed food lover but seeker of healthier options, I hope you enjoy these recipes as much as we did creating them!

LAURA AGAR WILSON

WHAT ARE GRAINS?

IN WITH THE OLD

WHAT ARE ANCIENT GRAINS?

The term "ancient grains" describes a number of grains or seeds that are enjoying a resurgence in popularity, but which in fact have been grown and eaten for hundreds of thousands of years by different cultures around the world.

A few of these grains, such as cornmeal (polenta) and wheat, are used readily in modern cooking. However, for others, it is only a matter of time until these grains become household names. As you will see from the recipes in this book, grains are much more than just a side dish. You can incorporate them into every meal – from breakfast to dinner, and (of course) dessert.

EAT LIKE AN EGYPTIAN

The history of ancient grains goes back thousands of years, when ancient civilizations relied on these grains as a source of energy and protein. Some grains, such as farro, are known to date back to the Egyptian era, when it was used in bread making.

Nowadays, grains are produced and harvested all across the world, and many can still be found in the areas from which they originated. Amaranth and quinoa originated, and are mostly grown, in South American regions; kamut and farro originated in Egypt; teff and barley are from Ethiopia; and millet is mainly from Africa and Asia.

Unlike many crops, these "newer" ancient grains are very much unchanged and free of hybridization (genetic modification), which is something most people are trying to avoid.

CARBOHYDRATE KINGS AND QUEENS

Whole grains are by far the best source of energy from a carbohydrate food. With many also high in fibre and protein (quinoa and amaranth are complete proteins, meaning that they are great alternatives to meat), these grains deliver the consistent energy we need, but they also come with a variety of nutrients and health benefits. Grains are low-fat, complex carbohydrates, making you feel satisfied for longer, and they can help to maintain a healthy weight by curbing craving and the desire to overeat.

Each grain contains many essential vitamins and nutrients, as well as antioxidants (for more information, see pages 18–19). Plus whole grains include disease-fighting phytonutrients (plant-based minerals that provide essential antioxidants), which are such a crucial part of a healthy diet.

Research is showing that, when enjoyed regularly, these grains can help control blood sugar and cholesterol levels and contribute towards reducing the likelihood of problems with high blood pressure, or strokes, heart disease, diabetes, and cancer.

QUALITY AND QUANTITY

Always buy your grains from a reliable source and, if purchasing them from a supermarket or health food shop, check the label. If you are using a whole grain, you want to make sure the whole grain, including the bran, is intact and that it has not been processed, which would remove a lot of the essential nutrients.

HEALTH AWARENESS

Many ancient grains are gluten-free and are completely safe for people who are gluten intolerant. If someone has mild gluten intolerance, they may also be able to eat some of the other grains, such as spelt, but for those with a more severe gluten intolerance, such as coeliac sufferers, only choose grains that are said to be from a dedicated gluten-free facility.

GRAINS FOR LITTLE PEOPLE

Grains are safe to eat for children over the age of 12 months. Government guidelines will vary, but most recommend that you do not feed children under the age of five only whole grains because they need to get nutrients from a wide variety of foods. When feeding grains to young children, it is best to soak the grains overnight. This will allow children to digest the grains and absorb the nutrients more easily.

THE GRAIN STORE
GLUTEN-FREE GRAINS

Whole grains contain all edible parts of the grain and are packed with nutrients including protein, fibre, B vitamins, antioxidants, and minerals. For anyone suffering from gluten intolerance, the following grains can play a huge part in a healthy, balanced diet.

QUINOA

Quinoa is a small round grain that has a slightly bitter flavour and a firm texture when cooked. Discovered by the Incas, quinoa was first grown thousands of years ago, and today the most widely cultivated varieties are white, red, and black. Due to its high oil content, quinoa is best stored in an airtight container in the fridge.

BUCKWHEAT

Originating from Asia, buckwheat is a fruit seed related to rhubarb and sorrel and has a unique triangular shape. Buckwheat is one of the healthiest, nuttiest, and most versatile whole grains. It is available unroasted or roasted. Stored correctly in a sealed container in a cool, dry place, whole buckwheat can last for up to 12 months.

TEFF

Teff is a tiny grain, similar in size to a poppy seed, and is available in a variety of colours, including white, red, and dark brown. Found predominantly in Ethiopia and Eritrea, teff can thrive in difficult conditions, including waterlogged soils and during droughts. Stored in a tightly sealed plastic or glass container, teff will keep for up to 12 months.

MiLLET

Millet is the name given to a group of small round grains, and the hulled variety is most commonly available. It was widely used in Asia before rice became the staple grain in the region. Millet becomes rancid fairly quickly, but, if kept in a sealed container, it will remain fresh for two months if stored in a cupboard, or for four months in the fridge.

CORNMEAL

Cornmeal, also often referred to as polenta, is believed to have been discovered by Native Americans circa 5000 BC. It is derived from ground, dried corn and its consistency can be fine, medium, or coarse. Cornmeal can retain its freshness for up to 12 months when sealed and stored in a cool, dry place.

SORGHUM

Native to Africa, Sorghum is a small, round grain, ranging in colour from white and brown to red and black. White sorghum is most commonly used and can be ground and substituted for wheat flour. Left whole, it makes fantastic popcorn. Stored in a container in a cool, dark place, it will keep for at least 12 months.

AMARANTH

Amaranth is a tiny seed with a nutty flavour that was discovered more than 8,000 years ago by the ancient Aztecs, who relied on it as one of their staple foods. Amaranth will lose its flavour and become bitter if it is stored in a warm location, but it will keep well for up to 12 months in a cool, dry cupboard.

GRAINS CONTAINING GLUTEN

For anyone who is sensitive to gluten, a protein found in wheat and other grains, such as barley, it is best to avoid the grains shown here. In general, when buying grains, make sure they are tightly sealed. If you notice a musty or oily aroma, then the grains are not in the best condition.

BULGUR WHEAT

Bulgur wheat is parboiled, dried, then cracked, and is pale brown in colour with an irregular shape. When cooked, it has a delicious nutty flavour and a chewy texture. It is popular in Middle Eastern and Mediterranean cuisines. This grain should be stored in an airtight container and keeps well in a cool, dry place for up to a year.

BARLEY

A fabulously versatile grain, barley has a long and interesting history originating in Ethiopia and South East Asia over 10,000 years ago. The most common form is pearl barley, which has the outer husk and bran layers removed. Barley can have a shelf life of up to one year if stored in an airtight container in a cool place.

KAMUT

Kamut is a trademark name for a type of khorasan grain, believed to have derived from ancient Egypt. It is a brown grain with a long shape, similar to basmati rice, that has a nutty flavour and a chewy texture when cooked. If stored in an airtight container away from heat and moisture, kamut may keep for over 12 months.

FREEKEH

Freekeh is an ancient Middle Eastern grain and is actually wheat that is harvested early, while the grains are still green. The kernels are roasted, dried, and rubbed, resulting in a slightly smoky flavour and nutty texture. The grain should be stored in a sealed jar and will retain its flavour and freshness for up to a year.

FARRO

Farro is the Italian name for emmer wheat, a hard wheat from western Asia. Similar in texture to pearl barley, farro is popular in Italy for its distinctive nutty roasted flavour and chewy texture. It is versatile and can be added to soups, risottos, and salads. Farro will keep for up to one year if stored in a sealed container in a cool, dark place.

WHEAT BERRiES

Wheat berries are not berries, but the whole kernels from a wheat plant with the husks removed, and are available as a hard or soft grain. They have a delicate, creamy, nutty flavour and are a light, reddish brown colour. Wheat berries can be ground into flour or used whole and should be stored in a cool, dry place.

SPELT

Originating in Iran and parts of southern Europe, spelt is a relative of wheat and is one of the oldest grains. It has an oval-like shape and a characteristic nutty flavour. This grain can be used whole or can be ground into flour. Stored in a cool, dry place and sealed tightly, spelt will remain fresh for at least 12 months.

PERFECTLY COOKED

To ensure perfect results when cooking grains, follow the steps on pages 20 and 22–23. Rinse grains as necessary and use a heavy-based saucepan with a lid to cook them in. Use the guides below to make sure that your grains are perfectly cooked.

◄ COOKED AMARANTH

Amaranth should be cooked one part grain to three parts boiling water, then simmered gently for about 25 minutes. Cooked amaranth is rather sticky, but remains crunchy on the outside and soft inside.

COOKED FREEKEH ▲

Freekeh is extremely easy to cook. The cooking times and liquid ratios vary depending on whether you are using wholegrain or cracked freekeh, so follow the directions on the pack.

COOKED BUCKWHEAT ►

Buckwheat should be rinsed thoroughly before cooking. Add one part buckwheat to two parts boiling water or stock and cook for about 12–15 minutes. It also cooks well by absorption or steaming methods.

◄ COOKED FARRO

Farro is available in different varieties, and the wholegrain kind takes longer to cook than semi-pearled or pearled. The easiest way to cook it is in boiling water (in a 1:2 ratio of grain to water) for approximately 15–20 minutes. Its chewy texture makes farro a fantastic substitute for rice or pasta.

COOKED KAMUT ▲

Pre-soaking kamut is optional but will significantly speed up the cooking process. Bring the measured water to the boil (use a 1:2 ratio of grain to water), add the drained, soaked grain, then cover, and simmer for 30–40 minutes. **Spelt** can be cooked in a similar way.

COOKED QUINOA ▶
Rinse quinoa before cooking, to remove the bitter coating. Boil for 10–15 minutes. The cooked grains quadruple in size and become translucent. **Millet** can be cooked similarly, but does not need rinsing.

FLOUR AND FLAKES

These flours and flakes contain the whole grain. Stored carefully and covered, they will keep for 3 months in a cool, dry place out of direct sunlight. Gluten-free flours produce crumblier baked goods, so it helps to add extra liquid.

AMARANTH FLOUR Amaranth flour is perfect for gluten-free cooking and baking, and can be used in cake, biscuit, bread, and pastry recipes.

BUCKWHEAT FLOUR Gluten-free and ideal for making pancakes, scones, and biscuits, this flour can be added to other flours for bread making.

◀ **COOKED SORGHUM**
Rinse sorghum before cooking, then cook in a ratio of one part grain to three parts water or stock. Bring to the boil in a pan with a tight-fitting lid, then simmer for up to an hour, until tender.

KAMUT FLOUR This wheat flour has a smooth, buttery, and nutty flavour. It can be substituted in any recipe that uses regular wheat flour.

MILLET FLAKES Wheat- and gluten-free, they are often used in muesli or porridge, or in crumbles and cookies for added texture.

COOKED TEFF ▶
Cooking teff depends on how it is being served. It can be cooked in boiling water or sprinkled over soups, salads, or baked goods, adding flavour and texture. It is also eaten as a cereal.

QUINOA FLAKES Made by flattening unprocessed, raw quinoa seeds, these are high in protein, gluten-free and can be used for muesli or porridge.

TEFF FLOUR A 100 per cent whole flour, it is creamy brown in colour with a unique sweet and malty flavour and is ideal for baking.

◀ **COOKED WHEAT BERRIES**
Cook wheat berries in a 1:2 ratio of grain to water. Add the grains to boiling water in a pan, cover, and simmer for about 60 minutes, until the grains are soft. Soaking wheat berries overnight can help to reduce the cooking time.

GRAIN POWER

Grains are an excellent source of protein, carbohydrates, fibre, and many minerals and vitamins. The information in this section shows how a portion of each grain (45g/1½oz of the dry grain) can contribute to the recommended daily intakes of these vital nutrients. The table below explains what the functions of each nutrient are in maintaining a healthy body.

KNOW YOUR NUTRIENTS

NUTRIENTS	GOOD FOR
Protein	general health and growth
Carbohydrates	providing energy
Calcium	bones and teeth; regulating muscle contractions
Fibre	digestion; preventing heart disease and diabetes
Iron	making red blood cells
Magnesium	muscle and nerve function; controlling glucose levels; regulating blood pressure
Phosphorus	bones and teeth; maintaining vital organs
Potassium	regulating blood pressure; keeping kidneys healthy
Sodium	muscles and nerves
Zinc	growth and development; taste and smell
Copper	maintaining vital organs; metabolism
Manganese	bones; producing collagen
Selenium	reproduction; metabolism; protecting against infection

VITAMINS	GOOD FOR
Thiamin (B1)	metabolism; processing energy
Riboflavin (B2)	building blood cells; metabolism
Niacin (B3)	processing energy; protecting against free radicals; metabolism
Pantothenic (B5)	processing energy; building hormones; immune system
Pyridoxine (B6)	proper growth; organ development; healthy blood; good cholesterol levels
Folic Acid (B9)	blood cells; regulating the nervous system (essential during pregnancy)
Vitamin C	blood cells; healing wounds

THE GOODIES IN GRAINS

The calorific content and amounts of protein, carbohydrates, fibre, and significant levels of minerals and vitamins are listed here per portion (45g/1½oz dry weight) of each grain featured in the book. The grains also contain traces of other nutrients.

CORNMEAL
Calories 163 **Protein** 3.65g
Carbohydrates 34.60g **Fibre** 3.3g

Good source of magnesium; phosphorus; manganese; selenium; Vitamins B2 and B3

QUINOA
Calories 166 **Protein** 6.35g
Carbohydrates 28.87g **Fibre** 3.2g

Good source of iron; copper; Vitamins B1 and B6

Excellent source of magnesium; phosphorus; manganese; folate

AMARANTH
Calories 167 **Protein** 6.10g
Carbohydrates 29.36g **Fibre** 3.0g

Good source of iron; copper; selenium; Vitamin B6

Excellent source of magnesium; phosphorus

Provides 50% of RDI of manganese

FARRO
Calories 162 **Protein** 5.74g
Carbohydrates 32.55g **Fibre** 4.4g

Good source of magnesium; zinc

Excellent source of Vitamin B3

SORGHUM
Calories 166 **Protein** 6.35g
Carbohydrates 28.87g **Fibre** 3.2g

Good source of phosphorus; Vitamin B6

Excellent source of magnesium

BARLEY
Calories 159 **Protein** 5.62g
Carbohydrates 33.7g **Fibre** 7.8g

Good source of magnesium; phosphorus; copper; Vitamin B3

Excellent source of manganese; selenium; Vitamin B1

FREEKEH
Calories 160 **Protein** 6.42g
Carbohydrates 32.14g **Fibre** 6.4g

Good source of calcium; magnesium; potassium; zinc; Vitamins B1 and B2

Excellent source of iron; copper

SPELT
Calories 166 **Protein** 6.35g
Carbohydrates 28.87g **Fibre** 3.2g

Good source of iron; magnesium; phosphorus; copper; manganese; Vitamins B1 and B3

Provides 50% of RDI of manganese

BUCKWHEAT
Calories 154 **Protein** 5.96g
Carbohydrates 32.18g **Fibre** 4.5g

Good source of phosphorus; Vitamins B2 and B3

Excellent source of magnesium; copper; manganese

KAMUT
Calories 152 **Protein** 6.54g
Carbohydrates 31.76g **Fibre** 5.0g

Good source of phosphorus; potassium; zinc; Vitamin B3

Excellent source of Vitamin B1

Provides 50% of RDI of manganese; selenium

TEFF
Calories 165 **Protein** 5.98g
Carbohydrates 31.59g **Fibre** 3.6g

Good source of iron; phosphorus; zinc; Vitamins B1 and B6

Excellent source of magnesium; copper

Provides 50% of RDI of Vitamin C and 100% of RDI of manganese

BULGUR WHEAT
Calories 154 **Protein** 5.53g
Carbohydrates 34.14g **Fibre** 8.2g

Good source of magnesium; phosphorus; Vitamin B3

Provides 50% of RDI of manganese

MILLET
Calories 170 **Protein** 4.96g
Carbohydrates 32.78g **Fibre** 3.8g

Good source of magnesium; phosphorus; copper; Vitamins B1 and B3

Excellent source of manganese

WHEAT BERRIES
Calories 163 **Protein** 6.70g
Carbohydrates 32.55g **Fibre** 5.74g

Good source of iron (white); magnesium; phosphorus; Vitamins B1 and B3

Excellent source of selenium

Provides 50% of RDI of manganese (red)

Good source = circa 10% of the recommended daily intake Excellent source = circa 20% of the recommended daily intake

BE PREPARED

Grains are easy to prepare, but each grain has a slightly different preparation method. The recipe will mention any extra steps needed to prepare the grain; some will take a few more steps than others. When reading a recipe, note which ones need extra time to rinse, soak, toast, pop, or cook the grain.

RiNSE

Most grains do not need rinsing, except quinoa, but it is beneficial. Run the grain under cold water in a fine mesh sieve immediately before cooking.

SOAK

Soak grains that take longer to cook. Place the grain in a bowl, cover with cold water, and leave it overnight. Drain and rinse before cooking.

POP

Heat a pan over a medium-high heat. Add a small amount of the grain. As it heats up, the grain will start to pop. Watch it carefully, so it doesn't burn.

ROAST

Roasting adds a nutty or crunchy taste. Spread the grain on a baking sheet and bake for about 5 minutes, or according to the recipe's instructions.

TOAST

Toasting can enhance a grain's flavour.
Heat a pan over a medium-high heat
and add the grain. Shake the pan
gently so that the grain turns
an even colour.

COOK THE PERFECT GRAIN

There are a variety of cooking methods you can choose from to cook your grain. It all depends on what equipment you own and what works best for you, but you can always rely on boiling any grain if you do not own a rice steamer or pressure cooker.

BOiL

1 For information on cooking times and liquid-to-grain ratio, see pages 16–17. To cook all grains, you can either bring the grain and liquid to the boil or add the grain to boiling water.

2 Reduce the heat and simmer until the grain is fully cooked. Some grains will absorb the water, and others will need to be drained after cooking.

USING A RICE STEAMER

An easy way to cook grains, the benefit of a rice steamer is that once you have added the liquid and grain, you can leave it to do its work. Instructions and timings for using individual steamers will vary, but the results are good.

USING A PRESSURE COOKER

This is ideal for cooking wheat berries, barley, spelt, and kamut, which all have longer cooking times. But all grains should cook in about half the time. Treat the grain as you would rice, but adjust the timing according to the grain.

STICKY MATTERS – A COUPLE OF HANDY TIPS

It takes a little while to get accustomed to cooking different grains and, as with rice and pasta, you may run into some common problems.

If your grains get stuck to the bottom of the saucepan, add a very small amount of water while the heat is on low and use a wooden spoon to loosen the grains. Do this until the water has been absorbed.

To soak up extra moisture, turn the heat off, drape a tea towel over the pan, and place the lid on top. Let it sit for another 5–10 minutes.

GRAIN TEASERS

Cooking with grains is simple and, in most cases, boiling them is enough, but some recipes call for different techniques, so the following instructions will explain some procedures in more detail and, hopefully, allow you to devise your own dishes.

MAKING GRANOLA

1 To prepare the granola, preheat the oven to 150°C (300°F/Gas 2), then mix the dry ingredients together in a large bowl. Pour over the wet mixture of honey (or maple syrup), oil and any additional ingredient, and mix well with a spoon until combined.

2 Place the granola mixture on a baking sheet and spread evenly. Bake for 30 minutes until crispy, then transfer to a plate and leave to cool.

MAKING POLENTA

1 Pour the measured water into a pan and bring to the boil, reduce the heat, then gradually add the weighed polenta, stirring continuously. Stir for a minute or two until it starts to thicken.

2 Reduce the heat and continue stirring until the polenta begins to come away from the sides of the pan. Polenta can take 45 minutes to cook, while instant varieties can be ready in about 5 minutes.

3 To use as slices, transfer the polenta to a greased baking tray and spread it with a spatula until it is level. Allow the polenta to stand for 30 minutes to cool and firm up, then cut into slices.

4 Once the polenta has been cut into slices, heat some oil and butter in a griddle pan over a medium heat, and fry the polenta for 2–3 minutes on each side, until golden.

MAKING RISOTTO

1 To prepare risotto, heat butter and oil in a large non-stick pan and gently fry the onions, and any additional vegetables, until soft. Add the grain, stirring continuously, until shiny and transparent.

2 Add white wine, if using, and simmer over a gentle heat until evaporated. Pour over the hot stock, a ladleful at a time, stirring the mixture with each addition until the stock is fully absorbed.

3 Reduce the heat and simmer the risotto for 30 minutes, stirring occasionally, adding liquid when required until the grain is cooked, but still firm. The risotto should be creamy and slightly wet.

4 Finally, stir in any remaining ingredients, such as grated Parmesan, butter, or fresh herbs. Allow the risotto to stand for 3–4 minutes, so that the flavours develop and the liquid is absorbed.

MAKING PATTIES

1 To prepare patties, place all the ingredients in a mixing bowl and bring the mixture together using a fork. Divide the mixture into equal portions and carefully roll into balls.

2 Using slightly wet hands, flatten the balls into rounds about 1.5–2cm (½–¾in) thick. Transfer the patties to a plate, cover with cling film, and leave in the fridge to firm up.

DRINKS AND SMOOTHIES

Add liquid to a blender, such as cow's, soya or almond milk, yogurt, or fruit juice. Then add your choice of fruit, vegetables, and cooked grains and blitz for 1 minute until smooth.

BATCH COOKING AND FREEZING

Batch cooking and freezing grain dishes is a great way to avoid waste and save money. You can freeze most dishes, but always cool them completely before freezing. Place them in a suitable container, leaving some space for expansion, and seal tightly to prevent freezer burn. Label with a date and description.

BREAKFAST AND BRUNCH

WHEAT BERRY BiRCHER MUESLi POTS

Perfect for spring or summer, these bircher muesli pots replace the traditional oats with wheat berries that add a delicious nutty flavour and texture.

SERVES 4 · PREP 25 MiNS, PLUS OVERNiGHT SOAKING AND COOLiNG · COOK 30 MiNS

120g (4¼oz) uncooked wheat berries

250g (9oz) blueberries

250g (9oz) strawberries, hulled

400g (14oz) plain yogurt

4 tbsp sunflower seeds, plus extra to serve

4 tbsp honey, plus extra to serve

1 Place the wheat berries in a large bowl, cover with water, and leave to soak overnight or for up to 8 hours. Then drain well, rinse under running water, and drain again.

2 Place the wheat berries in a large saucepan, cover with plenty of water, and bring to the boil. Then reduce the heat to a simmer, cover, and cook for 30 minutes or until the wheat berries are tender. Remove from the heat, drain any remaining water, and leave to cool completely.

3 Meanwhile, wash the blueberries and place them in a separate bowl. Wash the strawberries, hull, and cut them into thin slices. Add them to the blueberries and toss to mix. Once cooled, place the wheat berries, yogurt, sunflower seeds, and honey in a large bowl. Mix until well combined.

4 Divide half the wheat berry and yogurt mixture equally between 4 serving bowls, glasses, or jars. Top with a layer of half the strawberries and blueberries. Repeat the process adding one more layer of yogurt and fruit. Sprinkle over some sunflower seeds and add a drizzle of honey before serving.

GRAIN EXCHANGE

In place of the wheat berries, you could use any one of the following grains. Use the same amount as the wheat berries and see p16–17 for advice on cooking times.

buckwheat

kamut

farro

why not try...

Try adding **raspberries** and **blackberries** in place of the blueberries and strawberries.

BAKED BLUEBERRY AND SPELT OATMEAL

A healthy breakfast dish that feels like a treat. The spelt adds a nutty flavour and a crunchy, chewy texture to the oats that complement the sweet and savoury mixture of soft fruit and mixed nuts.

SERVES 6 · PREP 15 MINS, PLUS COOLING · COOK 1 HR 20 MINS

75g (2½oz) uncooked spelt

4 tsp extra virgin olive oil, plus extra for greasing

300g (10oz) blueberries

225g (8oz) rolled oats

1 tsp baking powder

¼ tsp ground cinnamon

¼ tsp grated nutmeg

pinch of salt

2 large eggs

500ml (16fl oz) whole milk or almond milk

1 tsp vanilla extract

3 tbsp maple syrup

2 tbsp mixed seeds, such as pumpkin, chia, and sunflower seeds

1 Place the spelt in a lidded saucepan, cover with 500ml (16fl oz) of water, and bring to the boil. Then reduce the heat to a simmer, cover, and cook for about 45 minutes, until most of the water has been absorbed. Remove from the heat, drain any remaining water, and rinse well under running water. Set aside to dry.

2 Preheat the oven to 180°C (350°F/Gas 4). Grease a 20 x 25cm (8 x10in) baking dish with a little oil. Spread out the blueberries in an even layer at the bottom of the dish. Place the oats, baking powder, cinnamon, nutmeg, and salt in a bowl. Add the spelt and mix until well combined. Place the eggs, milk, vanilla extract, maple syrup, and oil in a separate bowl and whisk to combine.

3 Add the wet mixture to the dry ingredients and mix until well combined. Spoon the mixture over the blueberries and spread it out in an even layer. Top with a layer of the mixed seeds and place in the oven. Bake for 30–35 minutes or until the top is golden brown and the oats are cooked. Remove from the heat and leave to cool slightly. Serve warm.

QUINOA AND POLENTA BREAKFAST MUFFINS
WITH FRIED EGGS, BACON, AND AVOCADO

Rich in whole grains, these deliciously savoury muffins make a perfect start to your day. Serve the muffins with eggs, bacon, and avocado for a filling and hearty breakfast.

SERVES 4 · PREP 10 MINS · COOK 20 MINS

1 tbsp light olive oil

4 large eggs

8 bacon rashers

large knob of butter, to serve

2 avocados, pitted and cut into thin slices, to serve

FOR THE BATTER

130g (4½oz) polenta

60g (2oz) wholemeal flour

150g (5½oz) prepared quinoa (see p22)

1 tbsp baking powder

½ tsp baking soda

¾ tsp sea salt

250ml (9fl oz) milk

3½ tbsp light olive oil

1 tbsp honey

3 large eggs

1 Preheat the oven to 200°C (400°F/Gas 6). Grease and line an 8-hole muffin tin with paper cases. For the batter, place the polenta, flour, quinoa, baking powder, baking soda, and salt in a large bowl and mix to combine.

2 In a separate bowl, whisk together the milk, oil, honey, and eggs until well combined. Then gently fold the liquid mixture into the dry ingredients and mix until just combined.

3 Divide the batter equally between the 8 muffin cases and transfer the tin to the oven. Bake for about 20 minutes or until a toothpick inserted into the centre comes out clean.

4 Meanwhile, heat the oil in a frying pan over a medium heat and fry the eggs. Then add the bacon rashers and fry until crisp. Split the muffins, top with some butter, and serve with the fried eggs, bacon, and avocado.

MiLLET AND TEFF SWEET POTATO WAFFLES
WiTH COCONUT YOGURT

The subtle combination of millet and teff flour creates fluffy, nutty waffles that are also gluten-free. The refreshing coconut milk yogurt neatly complements the tangy sweet potatoes making this tasty breakfast dairy-free as well.

MAKES 12 · PREP 15 MiNS, PLUS CHiLLiNG · COOK 50–55 MiNS

1 large sweet potato, about 400g (14oz), diced

a drizzle of olive oil

175g (6oz) teff flour

85g (3oz) millet flour

½ tsp salt

2 tsp baking powder

¼ tsp ground cinnamon

½ tsp grated nutmeg

60ml (2fl oz) coconut oil, room temperature, plus extra for greasing

3 eggs, lightly beaten

1 tsp vanilla extract

3 tbsp maple syrup, plus extra to serve

400g can coconut milk

1 tbsp shredded coconut, plus extra to serve

240ml tub coconut milk yogurt

1 Preheat the oven to 200°C (400°F/Gas 6). Place the sweet potatoes on a small baking sheet and drizzle with olive oil. Bake the sweet potatoes for about 30 minutes, until tender and cooked through. Remove from the heat and leave to cool. Once cooled, mash the potatoes with the back of a fork until smooth, then set aside.

2 Reduce the oven temperature to 130°C (250°F/Gas ½). Preheat the waffle maker or iron. Place both lots of flour, salt, baking powder, cinnamon, and nutmeg in a large bowl and mix well. In a separate bowl, place the coconut oil, eggs, vanilla extract, maple syrup, coconut milk, and mashed potatoes. Mix until well combined.

3 Add the wet mixture to the dry ingredients and stir well until the mixture is smooth and well incorporated. Lightly grease the waffle maker. Pour a small ladleful of the batter onto the waffle maker or iron and spread almost to the edge. Close the lid and bake until golden brown. Transfer to the heated oven and keep warm in a single layer while you make the rest of the waffles.

4 Meanwhile, place the coconut and yogurt in a large bowl and mix well to combine. Cover with cling film and chill in the fridge for about 15 minutes. Place warm waffles on plates and top with a scoop of the yogurt. Sprinkle over some shredded coconut, drizzle with maple syrup, and serve immediately.

AMERICAN-STYLE SOAKED BUCKWHEAT PANCAKES
WITH CHERRY ALMOND SAUCE

Buckwheat makes an incredible gluten-free flour and is even kinder on your digestion when soaked overnight. These fluffy and wholesome American-style pancakes are perfectly paired with a cherry almond sauce.

MAKES 8 PANCAKES · PREP 10 MINS, PLUS OVERNIGHT SOAKING · COOK 30 MINS

FOR THE BATTER

150g (5½oz) buckwheat flour

60ml (2fl oz) plain yogurt

200ml (7fl oz) milk

2 eggs

¾ tsp baking soda

¼ tsp baking powder

½ tsp vanilla extract

⅛ tsp salt

1–2 tbsp coconut oil, plus extra if needed

Greek yogurt, to serve

FOR THE SAUCE

350g (12oz) cherries, stoned

3 tbsp sugar

1 tsp almond extract

1 For the batter, place the flour, yogurt, and milk in a large bowl. Mix to combine, cover with a kitchen towel, and leave at room temperature for 8 hours or up to 24 hours.

2 Place the eggs, baking soda, baking powder, vanilla, and salt in a large bowl. Whisk lightly until well blended. Then gradually pour the egg mixture into the flour mixture and whisk until well combined.

3 Heat a large non-stick frying pan over a medium-high heat and add the oil once the pan is hot. Pour tablespoons of the batter into the pan, leaving space between them for the pancakes to spread. Each pancake should spread to about 15cm (6in) in diameter.

4 Cook the pancakes until small bubbles appear on the surface and the underside is firm. Then turn them over and cook for a further 1–2 minutes or until cooked through. Transfer the cooked pancakes to a warm oven. Continue cooking until all the batter is used up, adding more oil to the pan as needed.

5 For the sauce, place the cherries in a large, lidded saucepan and cover with 100ml (3½fl oz) water. Add the sugar and place the pan over a medium-high heat. Cover and simmer until the cherries have broken down. Then uncover and cook until the liquid becomes syrupy. Remove from the heat and stir in the almond extract. Serve the cherry almond sauce with the pancakes and Greek yogurt.

CRANBERRY, ORANGE, AND CHOCOLATE QUINOA BARS

The perfect breakfast on the go or handy snack, these sweet, chewy, and wholesome bars feel like a treat, but pack a big nutritional punch and will keep you full all morning.

MAKES 12 BARS · PREP 20 MINS, PLUS COOLING · COOK 5 MINS

120g (4¼oz) almonds, roughly chopped

120g (4¼oz) quinoa flakes

35g (1¼oz) sunflower seeds

35g (1¼oz) chia seeds

100g (3½oz) dried cranberries

125g (4½oz) puffed rice cereal

50g (1¾oz) dark chocolate chips

grated zest of 2 large oranges

85ml (2¾fl oz) coconut oil

120ml (4fl oz) clear honey

35g (1oz) light brown sugar

1 Place the almonds, quinoa flakes, sunflower seeds, chia seeds, dried cranberries, puffed rice cereal, chocolate chips, and orange zest in a bowl. Mix well with a wooden spoon and set aside. Grease and line a 20 x 25cm (8 x 10in) baking tin with greaseproof paper.

2 Heat the oil, honey, and sugar in a saucepan over a medium heat. Cook, stirring occasionally, for about 5 minutes or until the sugar has melted and the mixture is bubbling. Set aside to cool for about 2 minutes.

3 Pour the cooled honey mixture into the dry ingredients. Mix using a wooden spoon until well incorporated, making sure the chocolate chips have melted and are evenly combined. Spoon the mixture into the prepared baking tin. Press down firmly with the back of a wooden spoon to make a roughly even layer.

4 Place the baking tin in the fridge for at least 4 hours, to allow the mixture to cool and harden. Remove from the fridge, turn out on to a chopping board, and cut into bars. These can be stored in an airtight container in the fridge for up to 5 days.

GRAIN EXCHANGE

If you don't have quinoa flakes, then try using the same amount of **millet flakes** instead.

why not try...

Add **walnuts** instead of the almonds, **pumpkin seeds** instead of sunflower seeds, and **raisins** or **chopped dates** instead of the cranberries. In each case, use the same amount of the substitute ingredient as recommended in the recipe.

STRAWBERRY BARLEY SCONES

This British classic is given a wholegrain twist with the addition of barley. Use other berries instead of the strawberries, depending on the season.

MAKES 8 · PREP 20 MINS, PLUS COOLING · COOK 20 MINS

175g (6oz) barley flour	125g (4½oz) strawberries, finely chopped
150g (5½oz) wholewheat plain flour, plus extra for dusting	1 tsp vanilla extract
	1 large egg
½ tsp salt	75ml (2½fl oz) whole milk, plus extra for brushing
1 tbsp baking powder	
½ tsp baking soda	4 tbsp maple syrup
100g (3½oz) unsalted butter, chilled and diced	1 tbsp cane sugar

1 Preheat the oven to 200°C (400°F/Gas 6). Line a baking sheet with baking parchment. Place both lots of flour, the salt, baking powder, and baking soda in a large bowl. Mix well to combine. Then rub in the butter until the mixture resembles breadcrumbs. Add the strawberries and mix well.

2 Place the vanilla extract, egg, milk, and maple syrup in a separate bowl and whisk to combine. Add the wet mixture to the dry ingredients and mix until just combined. Be careful not to overmix.

3 On a well-floured surface, roll out the dough to a 1cm (½in) thick square, roughly 18cm (7in) in size. Then cut the dough into four equal-sized squares. Cut the squares diagonally, to form triangles, and transfer to the prepared baking sheet.

4 Brush the scones with milk, sprinkle over the sugar, and bake for 18–20 minutes, until turning golden. Remove from the heat and leave to cool on the baking sheet for 10 minutes. Then transfer to a wire rack to cool. Serve at room temperature.

CARAMELIZED AMARANTH PORRIDGE

Start the day off right, with a warm bowl of sweet porridge topped with syrupy caramelized bananas.

SERVES 4 · PREP 10 MINS · COOK 30 MINS

225g (8oz) uncooked amaranth	1 tsp lemon juice
	1 tsp ground cinnamon
60g (2oz) caster sugar	pinch of rock salt
3 ripe bananas, halved lengthways and sliced into 1cm (½in) pieces	1 tbsp unsalted butter
2 tbsp light soft brown sugar	

1 Place 675ml (1 pint) of water in a large, lidded saucepan and bring to the boil. Add the amaranth, cover, and reduce the heat to medium-low. Cook for about 20 minutes or until all the water has been absorbed. Add the caster sugar, mix well to combine, and remove from the heat.

2 Meanwhile, place the bananas, brown sugar, lemon juice, cinnamon, and salt in a large bowl. Mix gently to coat the bananas and form a syrupy mixture.

3 Melt the butter in a non-stick frying pan, swirling to coat the bottom. When the butter begins to bubble, add the banana mixture and cook, stirring occasionally, for 3–4 minutes or until the bananas are softened and begin to turn golden. Remove from the heat. Divide the amaranth between four bowls and top with the caramelized bananas. Serve immediately.

SORGHUM AND EGGS RANCHERO

This popular Mexican breakfast is given a hearty and healthy touch with the use of the nutrient-rich super-grain sorghum in place of the more usual rice. The spicy salsa and salty Manchego cheese are the perfect accompaniments.

SERVES 4 · PREP 10 MINS, PLUS STANDING · COOK 1 HR

100g (3½oz) uncooked sorghum

500ml (16fl oz) chicken stock

3 tbsp extra virgin olive oil, plus extra if needed

425g can black beans, drained and rinsed

½ teaspoon cumin

4 small corn tortillas

4 large eggs

2 avocados, pitted and diced

30g (1oz) Manchego cheese

handful of coriander leaves, roughly chopped, to garnish

FOR THE SALSA

3 tomatoes, grated

2–3 tbsp finely chopped onion

1 jalapeño, finely chopped

1 garlic clove, crushed

1–2 tbsp hot sauce

salt and freshly ground black pepper

1 Place the sorghum in a small saucepan, cover with the stock, and bring to the boil. Then reduce the heat to a simmer, cover, and cook for 45 minutes. Remove from the heat and leave to stand, covered, for about 10 minutes. Then drain any remaining water and set aside.

2 Meanwhile, for the salsa, place the tomatoes, onions, jalapeños, garlic, and hot sauce in a bowl. Season with a pinch of salt and some pepper and mix well. Heat 2 tablespoons of the oil in a small saucepan over a medium-low heat. Add the tomato mixture and cook for 2–3 minutes, until thickened and well combined. Remove from the heat and set aside.

3 In a separate pan, add the beans, cumin, and 3 tablespoons of water. Cook over a medium heat, stirring occasionally, until most of the water has evaporated and the beans are tender. Remove from the heat and roughly mash the beans with the back of a fork. Set aside.

4 Heat a large frying pan over a medium-low heat. Add the tortillas and warm through for about 2 minutes on each side. Remove from the heat and set aside. Wipe the pan with kitchen paper, add the remaining oil, and increase the heat to medium. Fry the eggs, one at a time, adding more oil to the pan if needed.

5 To assemble the dish, divide the tortillas between four serving plates. Top with equal quantities of the sorghum and one fried egg each. Divide the beans, salsa, and avocado equally between the plates. Sprinkle over the Manchego cheese, garnish with coriander, and serve immediately.

tomatoes

BACON, CHEESE, AND KAMUT FRITTATA

A hearty and filling portion in every slice, this traditional italian omelette is really nutritious and is given a brand new feel and taste with the inclusion of super-food kamut.

SERVES 4–6 · PREP 20 MINS · COOK 30 MINS

1 onion, finely chopped

6 bacon rashers, cut into bite-sized pieces

225g (8oz) spinach, roughly chopped

6 large eggs

100g (3½oz) freshly grated medium Cheddar cheese

200g (7oz) prepared kamut (see p22)

salt and freshly ground black pepper

1 Heat a large non-stick, ovenproof frying pan over a medium-high heat. Add the onions and bacon and cook for about 5 minutes, until the bacon is cooked and the onions are translucent.

2 Add the spinach to the pan and cook for about 5 minutes, until it wilts and reduces in volume. Remove from the heat and set aside.

3 Place the eggs and cheese in a large bowl or jug and whisk to combine. Add the kamut to the egg mixture and mix to combine. Then add the bacon and spinach mixture to the bowl and season. Whisk lightly to ensure that all the ingredients are well combined.

4 Return the pan to the stove and place over a medium-low heat. Pour the frittata mixture into the pan and cook for 10–15 minutes, without moving it, until the edges are set and the underside is cooked.

5 Set the grill at its highest setting and allow it to heat up for 5 minutes. Then place the pan under the grill for 2–3 minutes, until the frittata is golden brown on top. Remove from the heat and leave to rest for about 5 minutes. Slice the frittata into wedges and serve warm or at room temperature.

GRAIN EXCHANGE

This dish works well with a variety of similar grains. Try replacing the kamut with the same amount of any of the following.

wheat berries

spelt

farro

why not try...

Use the same amount of **tenderstem broccoli** in place of spinach. You can use it parboiled and drained or finely chopped and lightly sautéed.

MiLLET, BANANA, AND WALNUT BREAD

Sweet and bursting with fruit flavour, this banana bread benefits from the added millet, which provides it with a crunchy, nutty texture, as well as wholegrain goodness.

MAKES 900G (2LB) LOAF · PREP 20 MiNS · COOK 1 HR

240g (8½oz) wholemeal flour

100g (3½oz) light brown sugar

1 tsp baking soda

½ tsp baking powder

½ tsp cinnamon

75g (2½oz) walnuts, chopped

¼ tsp salt

2 bananas

2 large eggs

60ml (2fl oz) olive oil, plus extra for greasing

60ml (2fl oz) full-fat yogurt

150g (5½oz) prepared millet (see p22)

1 Preheat the oven to 180°C (350°F/Gas 4). Grease and line a 900g (2lb) loaf tin with baking parchment. Place the flour, sugar, baking soda, baking powder, cinnamon, walnuts, and salt in a bowl and mix well.

2 Place the bananas in a separate bowl and mash with a fork. Add the eggs, oil, and yogurt and mix until well incorporated. Then add the millet to the banana mixture and mix gently until combined.

3 Gradually fold the flour mixture into the banana and millet mixture until just combined. If the batter is over-mixed, the bread will be tough. Spoon the batter into the loaf tin and transfer to the oven.

4 Bake for 40 minutes, then remove from the oven and cover with foil. Return to the oven for a further 20 minutes or until a skewer inserted into the centre of the loaf comes out clean. Remove from the oven and leave to cool completely before serving.

GRAiN EXCHANGE

For a change, you could use the same amount of prepared **quinoa** in place of the millet.

why not try...

Try adding the same amount of **pecans** in place of the walnuts. You can also try using 115g (4oz) of **coconut palm sugar** instead of the light brown sugar.

HAM AND CHEESE EGG SCRAMBLE WITH VEGETABLE FARRO HASH

Simple to make, these classic scrambled eggs with ham and cheese get an extra vibrancy from the vegetables and farro, making it a complete meal that is perfect for a leisurely family breakfast.

SERVES 4 · PREP 10 MINS · COOK 20 MINS

2 tbsp olive oil

1 red onion, diced

200g (7oz) courgette, diced

1 red pepper, deseeded and diced

200g (7oz) prepared farro (see p22)

15g (½oz) basil, roughly chopped

salt and freshly ground black pepper

4 large eggs

60ml (2fl oz) milk

1 tbsp butter

115g (4oz) cooked ham, diced

115g (4oz) freshly grated Cheddar cheese

1 Heat the oil in a large frying pan over a medium heat. Add the onions, courgette, and red pepper. Cook for 8–10 minutes, stirring occasionally, until the vegetables are softened. Then add the farro and basil and stir to mix. Cook, stirring frequently, for a further 2 minutes or until heated through. Season to taste and remove from the heat. Set aside and keep warm.

2 Meanwhile, place the eggs and milk in a large bowl. Season with salt and pepper and whisk well to combine. Heat the butter in a non-stick frying pan over a medium heat. Pour in the egg mixture and cook, stirring occasionally, until cooked through. Then add the ham and cheese, stir to combine, and remove from the heat. Divide the egg scramble and vegetable farro hash equally between four plates and serve hot.

basil

PUMPKIN SPICED TEFF PORRIDGE

This rich spiced porridge made with teff is like autumn in a bowl – don't just save it for Halloween!

SERVES 2 · PREP 5 MINS · COOK 20 MINS

100g (3½oz) uncooked teff	1 tsp ground cinnamon
200g (7oz) pumpkin purée	½ tsp ground ginger
120ml (4fl oz) milk	20g (¾oz) pecans
4 tbsp maple syrup	

1 Place the teff and 400ml (14fl oz) of water in a large saucepan over a medium-high heat. Bring to a simmer and cook for about 15 minutes, stirring frequently, until all the water has been absorbed and the teff has a thick porridge-like consistency. Remove from the heat

2 Add the pumpkin purée, milk, maple syrup, cinnamon, and ginger. Mix well and return to a medium heat. Cook the porridge for 2 minutes, stirring constantly, until warmed through and well combined. Remove from the heat and sprinkle over the pecans. Serve hot.

SPELT BERRY BREAKFAST SALAD

Something a bit different for breakfast, this light salad is full of flavour matched with creamy Greek yogurt.

SERVES 4 · PREP 10 MINS · COOK 40 MINS

100g (3½oz) uncooked spelt	4 tbsp roughly chopped mint
100g (3½oz) blackberries	honey, to serve
100g (3½oz) raspberries	Greek yogurt, to serve

1 Place the spelt in a large saucepan, cover with plenty of water, and bring to the boil. Then reduce the heat to a simmer and cook for 30–40 minutes, until tender. Remove from the heat and drain any remaining water. Rinse the spelt under running cold water.

2 Place the spelt in a bowl. Add the blackberries, raspberries, and mint. Mix well to combine. Divide the salad between bowls and top with the honey. Serve immediately with Greek yogurt.

BLUEBERRY, AMARANTH, AND VANILLA MUFFINS

These tender breakfast muffins are made with nutty wholesome amaranth and dotted with ripe, sweet blueberries. Perfect when served warm with your morning coffee or even a glass of juice.

MAKES 12 MUFFINS · PREP 10 MINS · COOK 50 MINS

50g (1¾oz) uncooked amaranth

1 large egg

240ml (8fl oz) single cream

120ml (4fl oz) rapeseed oil, plus extra for greasing

250g (9oz) plain flour

75g (2½oz) granulated sugar

1 tbsp baking powder

½ tsp salt

1 tsp vanilla extract

225g (8oz) blueberries

1 Place the amaranth in a large saucepan, cover with water, and cook according to packet instructions. Remove from the heat, drain any remaining water, and leave to cool. Preheat the oven to 200°C (400°F/Gas 6). Grease and line a 12-hole muffin tin with paper cases.

2 Place the egg, single cream, and oil in a large bowl and beat together until combined. Add the flour, sugar, baking powder, salt, and vanilla extract to the mixture. Mix well to combine. Then add the blueberries and cooled amaranth and mix until evenly incorporated.

3 Divide the batter evenly between the paper cases. Transfer to the oven and bake for 25–30 minutes, until golden brown on top and a skewer inserted into the middle comes out clean. Leave the muffins in the tin to cool for 10 minutes. Then transfer to a wire rack to cool slightly. Serve warm.

GRAIN EXCHANGE

As an alternative, use the same amount of **quinoa** in place of the amaranth and cook it for 15 minutes.

why not try...

Instead of blueberries, try adding the same amount of **raspberries** or **dried cranberries**.

APPLE AND CINNAMON BREAKFAST FREEKEH

Crisp and tart apples and sweet apple juice combine with tender freekeh for a delicious and warming breakfast.

SERVES 4 · PREP 5 MINS · COOK 20 MINS

600ml (1 pint) apple juice

150g (5½oz) cracked freekeh

1 Granny Smith apple, cored and diced

30g (1oz) light brown sugar

ground cinnamon, to taste

1 Place the apple juice, freekeh, and apple pieces in a large saucepan. Mix well, set the pan over a medium heat, and bring to the boil.

2 Reduce the heat to medium-low, cover, and cook for 15–20 minutes, stirring occasionally, until the freekeh is tender.

3 Remove from the heat, stir in the sugar, and mix well to combine. Then add the cinnamon, as desired, and serve immediately.

CHOCOLATE AND HAZELNUT GRANOLA

For the sweet-toothed, this delicious variation on granola is the perfect start to the day.

MAKES ABOUT 800G (1³/₄LB) · PREP 15 MINS · COOK 15 MINS

125ml (4¼fl oz) honey

85ml (2¾fl oz) coconut oil

30g (1oz) cocoa powder

½ tsp salt

200g (7oz) rolled oats

200g (7oz) prepared buckwheat (see p22)

35g (1¼oz) pumpkin seeds

35g (1¼oz) sunflower seeds

100g (3½oz) hazelnuts, roughly chopped

1 Preheat the oven to 180°C (350°F/Gas 4). Line two baking trays with greaseproof paper and set aside. Place the honey in a large bowl. Melt the oil over a bowl of warm water and add to the honey. Then add the cocoa powder and salt to the bowl and mix well to combine.

2 Place the oats, buckwheat, pumpkin seeds, sunflower seeds, and hazelnuts in a separate bowl and mix to combine. Then add the honey, oil, and cocoa powder mixture to the dry ingredients and mix until well incorporated.

3 Divide the mixture evenly between the baking trays and spread it out to form a thin layer. Place in the oven and bake for 15 minutes. Remove from the oven and taste a little of the mixture to check if it is well toasted. Leave to cool in the tray. Serve with plain yogurt or fresh soft fruit.

BUCKWHEAT CRÊPES
WITH BRIE, APPLE, WALNUTS, AND PARMA HAM

These crêpes are based on the traditional Breton galette. The combination of fruit, cheese, and salty ham is a great blend of flavours and textures.

SERVES 4 · PREP 10 MINS · COOK 20 MINS

1–2 tbsp unsalted butter, room temperature, plus extra if needed

1 dessert apple, thinly sliced

225g (8oz) Brie cheese, cut into small pieces

60g (2oz) walnuts, roughly chopped

4 slices Parma ham, roughly chopped

FOR THE BATTER

1 tbsp unsalted butter, melted

75g (2½oz) buckwheat flour

150ml (5fl oz) whole milk

2 large eggs

1 Heat 1 tablespoon of the butter in a frying pan. Add the apples and cook for about 2 minutes, turning them over occasionally, until softened and lightly browned on both sides. Remove from the heat. Set aside and keep warm.

2 For the batter, place all the ingredients in a food processor and pulse until combined. Heat the remaining butter in a large, non-stick frying pan over a medium heat. Ladle 2–3 tablespoons of the batter into the centre of the pan. Tip the pan or use the back of the ladle to swirl the batter to coat the bottom of the pan and form a thin layer.

3 Cook the crêpe for 2 minutes or until the edges start to curl up and it is crisp and lightly browned underneath. Flip the crêpe over, top with one-quarter of the Brie, and cook for 1–2 minutes. Remove from the heat, transfer to a plate, and keep warm.

4 Repeat with the remaining batter, adding more butter to the pan if needed. Place the crêpes on serving plates and top each with one-quarter of the apples, walnuts, and Parma ham. Then fold them in half, tuck in the sides, and serve warm.

dessert apple

SPINACH AND ARTICHOKE QUICHE WITH AN AMARANTH CRUST

This tasty quiche uses amaranth flour for a delicious gluten-free and vegan crust and is ideal for a healthy and filling brunch. For best results, use artichokes that have been preserved in oil instead of those canned in water or brine.

SERVES 6 · PREP 20 MINS · COOK 50 MINS

FOR THE PASTRY

70g (2¼oz) amaranth flour

45g (1½oz) tapioca flour or cornflour

30g (1oz) ground almonds

¼ tsp salt

3 tbsp sunflower oil

FOR THE FILLING

1 tbsp olive oil

1 garlic clove, crushed

110g (3¾oz) onion, finely chopped

140g (5oz) spinach

4–5 artichoke hearts, drained and roughly chopped

60g (2oz) goat's cheese

FOR THE CUSTARD

2 large eggs

2 egg yolks

250ml (9fl oz) whole milk

salt and freshly ground black pepper

1 Preheat the oven to 200°C (400°F/Gas 6). Grease a 22cm (9in) loose-bottomed flan tin and set aside. For the pastry, place both lots of flour, almonds, and salt in a large bowl and mix well until combined. In a small bowl, whisk together the oil and 3 tablespoons of water. Make a well in the centre of the dry ingredients and pour the oil mixture in. Bring together to form a light and sticky dough, adding more water, a little at a time, if needed.

2 Roll out the dough between two sheets of cling film and use to line the prepared tin, making sure it forms a good side to the case. Prick the bottom of the pastry with a fork. Place in the oven and blind bake for about 10 minutes. Then remove from the heat and set aside. Reduce the oven temperature to 180°C (350°F/Gas 4).

3 For the filling, heat the oil in a large saucepan over a medium heat. Add the garlic and onions and cook for about 3–5 minutes or until the onions are translucent. Then add the spinach and cook for a further 2–3 minutes or until it has wilted. Remove from the heat and set aside.

4 For the custard, place the eggs, yolks, and milk in a large bowl. Season with ¼ teaspoon salt and a good grinding of pepper. Whisk until well combined. Spoon the onion and spinach mixture into the pastry case, making sure it covers the bottom. Spread out the artichoke hearts on top in a single layer and pour over the custard. Crumble the cheese and sprinkle over the custard.

5 Bake the quiche in the oven for about 40 minutes or until the custard has set and the top is golden. Remove from the heat and leave to cool slightly before cutting into wedges to serve. This quiche can be served warm or at room temperature.

NUTRITIOUS SOUPS

BEETROOT AND BUCKWHEAT SOUP
WITH LEMON YOGURT SAUCE

A vibrant and soothing soup, the contrasting flavours of the beetroot and tangy yogurt sauce are perfectly paired with the buckwheat for an ideal lunch or light dinner.

SERVES 4 · PREP 15 MINS · COOK 50 MINS

1 tbsp light olive oil

1 onion, finely chopped

750g (1lb 10oz) beetroot, trimmed and cut into small chunks

500ml (16fl oz) vegetable stock

400g can chopped tomatoes

salt and freshly ground black pepper

200g (7oz) prepared buckwheat (see p22)

handful of rosemary leaves

FOR THE SAUCE

250g (9oz) plain yogurt

juice of 1 lemon

1 Heat the oil in a large saucepan over a medium heat. Add the onion and cook for about 5 minutes, stirring frequently, until translucent. Then add the beetroot and stock. Bring the mixture to a simmer and cook for 30–40 minutes, until the beetroot is tender.

2 Add the tomatoes to the pan and cook for 2–3 minutes. Transfer the soup to a food processor and pulse until it reaches a smooth consistency. Season to taste, if needed. Pour the soup back into the pan and heat through over a low heat for 2–3 minutes. Remove from the heat.

3 For the sauce, place the ingredients in a bowl and mix to combine. Divide the soup between four bowls and top with the sauce. Then add equal quantities of the buckwheat, garnish with rosemary, and serve hot.

GRAIN EXCHANGE
Try replacing the buckwheat with the same amount of prepared sorghum or millet.

millet

sorghum

CREAMY GREEN SOUP WiTH WHEAT BERRiES

This gorgeous green soup is made extra creamy with the dairy-free addition of cannellini beans. The wholesome wheat berries give this soup an added heartiness and texture.

SERVES 4 · PREP 15 MiNS · COOK 30 MiNS

1 tbsp light olive oil

1 onion, finely chopped

2 garlic cloves, crushed

4 leeks, trimmed and finely sliced

500g (1lb 2oz) spring greens, stems removed and finely sliced

750ml (1¼ pints) vegetable stock

2 x 400g can cooked cannellini beans, drained

salt and freshly ground black pepper

400g (14oz) prepared and cooled wheat berries (see p22)

1 Heat the oil in a large saucepan over a medium heat. Add the onions and garlic and cook, stirring occasionally, for about 5 minutes.

2 Add the leeks to the pan and cook for about 10 minutes, stirring occasionally, until softened. Then add the spring greens and cook for a further 2–3 minutes or until they wilt.

3 Pour in the vegetable stock, bring to the boil, and allow the soup to simmer for about 10 minutes. Then add the cannellini beans to the pan and stir lightly to mix. Transfer the soup to a food processor and pulse until it reaches a smooth consistency. Season to taste, if needed.

4 Return the soup to the pan and place over a medium heat for 2–3 minutes to heat through. Then stir in the wheat berries and remove from the heat. Ladle into soup bowls, season with pepper, and serve hot.

GRAiN EXCHANGE
Instead of the wheat berries, try using the same amount of any one of the following grains.

barley

kamut

farro

why not try...

Use the same amount of **kale** (stalks removed) or **cabbage** in place of the spring greens.

SPRING VEGETABLE AND SORGHUM MINESTRONE
WITH PESTO

This refreshing soup is also full of goodness. Packed with flavour, it makes the best of fresh spring vegetables and wholesome sorghum and can be enjoyed on a warm or cool day alike.

SERVES 4 · PREP 15 MINS · COOK 1 HR 25 MINS

4 tbsp extra virgin olive oil

1 small fennel bulb, white and green parts only, diced

1 spring onion, diced

6 garlic cloves, thinly sliced

1 white potato, diced

1 tsp dried thyme

¼ tsp chilli flakes (optional)

salt and freshly ground black pepper

100g (3½oz) uncooked sorghum

400g can cannellini beans, drained

100g (3½oz) leafy greens, such as kale, spinach, and pak choi

FOR THE PESTO

large bunch of basil

1 small garlic clove, crushed

40g (1½oz) toasted pine nuts

40g (1½oz) freshly grated Parmesan cheese

120ml (4fl oz) extra virgin olive oil

1 Heat the oil in a large, heavy-based soup pot over a medium heat. Add the fennel and onions and cook for 10 minutes or until softened. Then add the garlic, potatoes, thyme, and chilli flakes. Season with ½ teaspoon salt, stir to mix, and cook for a further 2–3 minutes.

2 Add the sorghum and pour over 2 litres (3½ pints) of water. Bring to the boil, then reduce the heat to a simmer. Cook for about 40 minutes. Then add the beans, stir to mix, and cook for a further 20 minutes. Season to taste and cook for a further 2 minutes if the soup seems too watery. Add the greens, stir well, and cook for 5 minutes or until they have just about wilted. Remove from the heat.

3 For the pesto, place all the ingredients, except the oil, in a food processor. Pulse until roughly chopped and well combined. Then add the oil in a slow stream and pulse until emulsified. Taste, adding seasoning if needed. Ladle the soup into bowls and top with a spoonful of pesto. Serve hot.

SUMMER PEA, MiNT, AND AVOCADO SOUP WiTH QUiNOA

This light and creamy chilled soup is enhanced with the addition of the nutty flavoured and protein-packed quinoa. Quick and easy to prepare, it makes the perfect summer lunch.

SERVES 4 · PREP 10 MiNS · COOK 25 MiNS

50g (1¾oz) uncooked quinoa

2 avocados, pitted

500g (1lb 2oz) frozen peas

20g (¾oz) chopped mint, plus extra to garnish

1 litre (1¾ pints) unsweetened almond milk

1 Rinse the quinoa under running water, drain, and place in a lidded saucepan. Cover with 250ml (9fl oz) of water and bring to the boil.

2 Reduce the heat to a simmer, cover, and cook for 15–20 minutes or until almost all the liquid has been absorbed and the quinoa is fluffy. Remove from the heat, drain any remaining water, and set aside to cool.

3 Scoop out the flesh from the avocados and place in a food processor. Add the peas, mint, and half the milk and pulse until smooth. Then add the remaining milk and pulse until fully blended.

4 Divide the soup equally between four soup bowls. Top with equal quantities of the cooled quinoa. Garnish with some mint and serve immediately.

GRAiN EXCHANGE

You could use the same amount of barley or spelt in place of the quinoa.

spelt

barley

ROASTED TOMATO AND RED PEPPER SOUP WITH FARRO

This tangy version of the classic tomato soup is given a nutritional boost with the use of farro.

SERVES 4 · PREP 15 MINS, PLUS SOAKING · COOK 1 HR 10 MINS

150g (5½oz) uncooked farro

800g (1¾lb) tomatoes, quartered

3 red peppers, deseeded and roughly chopped

1 onion, roughly chopped

4 garlic cloves, crushed

3 tbsp light olive oil

500ml (16fl oz) vegetable stock

salt and freshly ground black pepper

4 tbsp chopped basil

1 Place the farro in a large bowl, cover with water, and leave to soak for 8 hours or for up to 12 hours. Then drain, rinse under running water, and drain well again. Place the farro in a saucepan and cover with water. Bring to the boil, then reduce the heat to a simmer, and cook for 30 minutes or until tender, but still with some bite. Remove from the heat.

2 Preheat the oven to 180°C (350°F/Gas 4). Place the tomatoes, red peppers, onions, and garlic in a baking tray, drizzle over the oil, and toss to coat. Place the tray in the oven and roast the vegetables for 45 minutes or until soft and slightly caramelized. Remove from the heat.

3 Transfer the vegetable mixture, along with any juices in the tray, to a food processor and pulse until smooth. Then add the stock, a little at a time, and pulse until it is well combined and reaches a soup-like consistency. Pour the soup into a pan and place over a low heat. Add the farro, stir to mix, and heat through for about 5 minutes. Season to taste, garnish with basil, and serve warm.

CHIPOTLE SWEET POTATO SOUP

Creamy and rich sweet potatoes and chipotle chillies are perfectly combined for a spicy twist to this popular soup.

SERVES 4 · PREP 10 MINS · COOK 1 HR 10 MINS

1 tbsp olive oil

1 sweet onion, diced

2 garlic cloves, crushed

2 chipotle chillies in 2 tbsp adobo sauce, finely chopped

950ml (1½ pints) low-sodium vegetable stock

450g (1lb) sweet potatoes, cut into 2.5cm (1in) cubes

1 tbsp honey

55g (1¾oz) uncooked freekeh

salt and freshly ground black pepper

1 Heat the oil in a Dutch oven or a large casserole over a medium heat. Add the onions and garlic and sauté for 3–5 minutes or until the onions are lightly browned. Then stir in the chipotle chillies and adobo sauce. Mix well to combine.

2 Add the stock, sweet potatoes, and honey. Stir to mix and bring the mixture to the boil. Then reduce the heat to medium-low, cover, and cook for about 30 minutes. Remove from the heat.

3 Use a hand-held blender to process the mixture to a purée. Stir in the freekeh and place over a medium-low heat and cook, stirring occasionally, for a further 30 minutes. Remove from the heat. Season to taste and serve immediately.

CREAMY MUSHROOM BARLEY SOUP

Keep some dried mushrooms and barley in your store cupboard so you can prepare this easy soup without much effort. Bursting with the flavours of dried herbs and white wine, it is filling enough to eat on its own and is an excellent winter soup.

SERVES 4–6 · PREP 10 MINS, PLUS SOAKING · COOK 1 HR

30g (1oz) mixed, dried porcini and shiitake mushrooms

100g (3½oz) uncooked barley

pinch of salt

1 tbsp unsalted butter

2 tbsp olive oil

1 onion, diced

2 garlic cloves, crushed

1 tsp dried thyme

1 tsp dried rosemary

½ tsp sea salt

190g (6½oz) chestnut mushrooms, thinly sliced lengthways

190ml (6½fl oz) dry white wine

950ml (1½ pints) low-sodium chicken stock

2 tbsp plain flour

120g (4¼oz) Greek yogurt, room temperature

1 tbsp roughly chopped chives, to garnish

1 Place the dried mushrooms in a large bowl and cover with 500ml (16fl oz) of warm water. Leave to soak for 30 minutes. Then drain the mushrooms and reserve the water. Roughly chop the mushrooms and set aside.

2 Place the barley in a large, lidded saucepan and cover with 375ml (13fl oz) of water. Add a pinch of salt and bring to the boil. Then reduce the heat to a simmer, cover, and cook for 45 minutes or until the barley is tender and all the liquid has been absorbed. Remove from the heat. Cover and set aside.

3 Meanwhile, heat the butter and oil in a large, heavy-based pot over a medium heat. Add the onions and cook for 2–3 minutes, stirring frequently, until soft and translucent. Then add the garlic, thyme, rosemary, and sea salt and stir to mix. Cook, stirring frequently, for a further 2 minutes.

4 Add the porcini, shiitake, and chestnut mushrooms. Cook, stirring frequently, for about 5 minutes or until the mushrooms have softened and are starting to brown. Then add the wine, stir to coat, and cook for about 10 minutes until it has evaporated.

5 Add the stock to the pot and stir to mix. Bring to the boil, then reduce the heat to a simmer, and cook for 5 minutes. Transfer 120ml (4fl oz) of the liquid to a bowl. Add the flour and whisk until well combined and smooth. Pour the mixture back into the soup, stir to combine, and cook for a further 20–25 minutes.

6 Add in the barley and cook, stirring occasionally, for 5 minutes. Remove from the heat. Place the yogurt in a bowl and pour over 1 tablespoon of the soup. Mix well to combine and stir into the soup. Mix until evenly incorporated. Garnish with chives and serve warm.

SWEET POTATO AND PEANUT SOUP WITH TEFF

Inspired by the flavours of West African cuisine, this sweet and spicy soup contains a hint of peanut. The addition of teff gives the dish a light, earthy flavour and a unique texture.

SERVES 6–8 · PREP 15 MINS · COOK 45 MINS

100g (3½oz) uncooked teff

1 tbsp light olive oil

1 onion, finely chopped

2 garlic cloves, finely chopped

1 tbsp ground cumin

400g can chopped tomatoes

700g (1lb 8oz) sweet potatoes, unpeeled and cut into cubes

1 litre (1¾ pints) vegetable stock

100g (3½oz) smooth peanut butter

salt and freshly ground black pepper

200g (7oz) plain yogurt, to serve

6 tbsp roughly chopped coriander leaves, to garnish

1 Place 400ml (14fl oz) of water in a large saucepan and bring to the boil. Add the teff and reduce the heat to a simmer. Cook for 10 minutes, stirring constantly, until all the water has been absorbed. Then remove from the heat and set aside.

2 Meanwhile, heat the oil in a large saucepan over a medium heat. Add the onions and garlic and sauté for about 5 minutes or until the onions have softened. Then add the cumin and sauté for a further 2 minutes.

3 Add the tomatoes, sweet potatoes, and stock to the pan and reduce the heat to a simmer. Cover and cook for 30 minutes or until the potatoes are soft. Remove from the heat and use a hand-held blender to process the soup until smooth. Then add the peanut butter and process until fully incorporated.

4 Add the teff to the soup and stir through. Return the pan to a medium heat and warm through for 2–3 minutes. Remove from the heat and season to taste, if needed. Ladle into soup bowls and top with a spoonful of yogurt. Sprinkle over the coriander and serve hot.

CHUNKY BUTTERNUT SQUASH AND BARLEY SOUP

The sweet and earthy flavour of orange-fleshed butternut squash shines through in this chunky soup, pepped up by just a hint of ginger and cinnamon. You can enjoy a bowl of this warming soup on the chilliest of autumn days.

SERVES 4 · PREP 10 MINS · COOK 50 MINS

- 100g (3½oz) uncooked pearl barley
- 2 tbsp olive oil
- 1 onion, diced
- salt and freshly ground black pepper
- 2 carrots, sliced into thin rounds
- 1 apple, cored and diced
- 1 red pepper, deseeded and diced
- 1 butternut squash, about 900g (2lb), deseeded and cut into cubes
- 1 litre (1¾ pints) vegetable stock
- 1 tsp ground cinnamon
- 1 tsp ground ginger
- 1 tsp sweet paprika

1 Place the barley in a large saucepan, cover with 350ml (12fl oz) of water, and bring to the boil. Reduce the heat to medium-low and cook for 25–30 minutes, or until tender. Then remove from the heat and drain any remaining water. Set aside.

2 Meanwhile, heat the olive oil in a large Dutch oven or saucepan over a medium heat. Add the onions and season with a pinch of salt. Cook for about 8 minutes, stirring frequently, until they start to get translucent. Then add the carrots, apples, red pepper, and butternut squash. Stir to mix and pour over the vegetable stock. Cover and cook, stirring occasionally, for about 30 minutes.

3 Add the cinnamon, ginger, and paprika. Cook for a further 10 minutes. Remove from the heat and take out about 150g (5½oz) of the vegetables with a slotted spoon and set aside. Use a hand-held blender to pulse the remaining mixture until it forms a smooth purée. Add the barley and reserved vegetables, season to taste, and mix well. Serve immediately.

red peppers

INDIAN SPICED RED LENTIL AND KAMUT SOUP

Lentils are one of the healthiest pulses, providing a great source of protein and iron. This lightly spiced warming soup also benefits from the flavour of the kamut and is perfect for cold winter days.

SERVES 4-6 · PREP 20 MINS · COOK 40 MINS

1 tbsp light olive oil

1 large onion, finely chopped

1 leek, trimmed and finely chopped

5cm (2in) piece of fresh root ginger, finely chopped

2 tsp mild curry powder

4 carrots, unpeeled and roughly chopped

300g (10oz) red lentils

300g (10oz) uncooked kamut

1.5 litres (2¾ pints) hot vegetable stock, plus extra if needed

salt and freshly ground black pepper

1 Heat the oil in a large saucepan over a medium heat. Add the onions and leeks and sauté for about 5 minutes. Then add the ginger and curry powder and stir to mix, adding a little water to the pan if they start to stick. Add the carrots, red lentils, and kamut to the pan and stir to mix.

2 Pour in 1 litre (1¾ pints) of the stock, reserving the rest. Cover, reduce the heat to a simmer, and cook for 30 minutes or until the lentils have broken down, the kamut is tender, and the carrots are cooked through. Check the soup occasionally and add more stock as needed.

3 Remove from the heat and use a hand-held blender to process the soup until it reaches a chunky texture, adding more stock if necessary. Taste and season with salt and pepper. Stir well to combine and serve warm.

leeks

WINTER VEGETABLE SOUP WITH BACON AND BARLEY

This delicious combination of root vegetables, winter greens, and fluffy, wholesome barley makes a filling dish and a truly comforting meal on a cold winter day.

SERVES 4 · PREP 10 MINS · COOK 55 MINS

- 1 tbsp light olive oil
- 1 onion, finely sliced
- 1 carrot, diced
- 1 parsnip, diced
- 1 small swede, about 250g (9oz), diced
- 200g (7oz) pearl barley, rinsed
- 1.5 litres (2¾ pints) vegetable stock
- 8 unsmoked bacon rashers, cut into bite-sized pieces
- 50g (1¾oz) kale, roughly chopped
- salt and freshly ground black pepper

1 Heat the oil in a large saucepan over a medium heat. Add the onion and cook for about 5 minutes, stirring occasionally, until softened. Then add the carrot, parsnip, and swede and cook for a further 5 minutes.

2 Add the barley and stock. Stir well and reduce the heat to a simmer. Cover, leaving the lid a little ajar, and cook for 30–40 minutes or until the vegetables and barley are tender.

3 Meanwhile, heat a small non-stick frying pan over a medium-high heat. Add the bacon and fry for about 5 minutes or until crispy. Remove from the heat and set aside.

4 Stir the kale into the soup and cook for a further 2–3 minutes or until the leaves have wilted. Remove from the heat, season to taste, and stir in the bacon. Ladle the soup into bowls and serve hot.

GRAIN EXCHANGE

For a variation, try using the same amount of any one of the following grains in place of the barley.

wheat berries

farro

spelt

why not try..

Try using the same amount of **cabbage** as the kale.

CHICKEN SOUP WITH SPELT

Using a good-quality chicken, preferably a free-range one, and making the stock from scratch will really ensure that you get the best flavour in this soup, which is boosted by the addition of the herbs.

SERVES 4–6 · PREP 20 MINS, PLUS OVERNIGHT SOAKING AND CHILLING · COOK 3 HRS

1 whole roasted chicken, about 1kg (2¼lb)

200g (7oz) uncooked spelt, soaked overnight

1 tbsp light olive oil

1 onion, finely chopped

2 garlic cloves, crushed

4 celery sticks, finely chopped

2 carrots, chopped into bite-sized pieces

2 potatoes, chopped into bite-sized pieces

½ tsp dried sage

½ tsp dried thyme

½ tsp dried rosemary

salt and freshly ground black pepper

4 tbsp chopped flat-leaf parsley

FOR THE STOCK

1 onion, finely chopped

2 garlic cloves chopped

2 celery sticks, finely chopped

1 tbsp apple cider vinegar

1 Place the chicken on a clean work surface. Use two forks to roughly shred the meat from the bones and place in a large bowl. Place the bowl in the fridge and leave to chill. Reserve the bones. Drain the spelt, rinse under running water, and drain well again. Set aside.

2 For the stock, place the bones in a large, lidded saucepan and cover with 2 litres (3½ pints) of water. Add the onions, garlic, celery, and vinegar. Season with ½ teaspoon of salt, cover, and simmer for at least 2 hours. Remove from the heat and skim away any fat that rises to the surface. Strain the stock into a large pan, discarding the bones and vegetables, and set aside.

3 Heat the oil in a large soup pot over a medium heat. Add the onions, garlic, and celery. Cook for about 5 minutes, stirring frequently, until the onion and celery have softened. Then add the carrots, potatoes, and spelt. Stir to combine.

4 Add the strained stock to the pan, cover, and simmer for 40 minutes or until the spelt is tender. Then add the sage, thyme, rosemary, and shredded chicken. Simmer the soup for a further 10 minutes or until the vegetables are cooked and the chicken has warmed through. Remove from the heat and season to taste, if needed. Garnish with parsley and serve immediately.

flat-leaf parsley

CREAMY CAULIFLOWER AND BULGUR WHEAT SOUP

A double whammy of Cheddar and Parmesan cheese really lifts this soup. The cauliflower is a classic foil for the cheese and, together with the bulgur wheat, gives the soup a lovely rich texture.

SERVES 4-6 · PREP 5 MiNS · COOK 30 MiNS

1 tbsp olive oil

1 onion, finely chopped

1 cauliflower, about 300g (10oz), cut into florets

200g (7oz) uncooked bulgur wheat

1.2 litres (2 pints) hot chicken stock

250ml (9fl oz) whole milk

140g (5oz) freshly grated medium Cheddar cheese

20g (¾oz) freshly grated Parmesan cheese

salt and freshly ground black pepper

1 Heat the oil in a large saucepan over a medium heat. Add the onion and sauté for about 5 minutes or until softened. Then add the cauliflower, bulgur wheat, and stock.

2 Cover, reduce the heat to a simmer, and cook for 20–25 minutes or until the cauliflower is tender. Then remove from the heat and use a hand-held blender to process the soup until smooth.

3 Return the soup to a low heat. Add the milk in a slow stream, stirring constantly to combine. Then add both lots of cheese, a little at a time, stirring constantly until the cheese has melted and is well combined. Remove from the heat and season to taste. Serve warm.

cauliflower

CELERIAC AND APPLE SOUP WITH POLENTA CROUTONS

Celeriac, or celery root, is the nutritious cousin of the popular parsnip. Blending it with apple makes a perfect combination, with the fruit adding a tangy sweetness to the hearty root vegetable soup.

SERVES 4-6 · PREP 10 MINS, PLUS CHILLING · COOK 55 MINS

FOR THE CROUTONS

salt and freshly ground
  black pepper

150g (5½oz) quick-cook
  polenta

2 sprigs of rosemary,
  finely chopped

2 tbsp olive oil

FOR THE SOUP

2–3 tbsp olive oil

2 celeriac, tops removed,
  peeled and diced

1 white potato, such as Cara
  or Maris Piper, diced

2 green apples,
  cored and diced

6 spring onions, white parts
  diced and green parts
  reserved to garnish

salt and freshly ground
  white pepper

60–120g (2–4¼oz) freshly
  grated Gruyère cheese

1 For the croutons, place 750ml (1¼ pints) of water in a saucepan. Add ¼ teaspoon of salt and bring to the boil. Then add the polenta, a little at a time, whisking continuously. Reduce the heat to low and cook for about 3 minutes, whisking continuously, until it has thickened. Remove from the heat.

2 Line a baking tray with greaseproof paper and set aside. Season the polenta with black pepper, add the rosemary and oil, and mix to combine. Spoon the mixture into the prepared baking tray and spread it out to form a 5mm (¼in) thick even layer. Place in the fridge and chill for 2 hours or until it firms up.

3 For the soup, heat the oil in a large, lidded saucepan over a medium heat. Add the celeriac, potatoes, apples, and onions. Cook for 8 minutes, stirring, until the celeriac and apples are soft, but not brown. Season with salt and white pepper, add 1.5 litres (2¾ pints) of water, and bring to the boil. Reduce the heat to a simmer, cover, and cook for 30–40 minutes. Remove from the heat and process the mixture with a hand-held blender, until reduced to a smooth purée. Season to taste, if needed.

4 Set the grill at its medium setting. Remove the polenta from the tray and cut it into four (or six) 5cm (2in) squares. Place them on a lined baking tray, sprinkle over the Gruyère cheese, and grill for about 3 minutes or until the cheese has melted and has started to brown. Ladle the soup into bowls and top with the croutons. Garnish with the reserved spring onions and serve immediately.

THAi CURRY, TOMATO, AND VEGETABLE SOUP WiTH FARRO

Tomato soup takes on a whole new life in this recipe, when mixed with Thai curry paste and a variety of fresh vegetables. The addition of farro gives just the right amount of bulk to this satisfying soup.

SERVES 4 · PREP 10 MiNS · COOK 1 HR 30 MiNS

- 75g (2½oz) uncooked farro
- 400g can light coconut milk
- 200ml (7fl oz) vegetable stock
- 175g (6oz) tomato purée
- 2 tbsp Thai red curry paste
- 1 tbsp light brown sugar
- 1 tbsp extra virgin olive oil
- 2 leeks, white and light green parts only, chopped
- 1 green pepper, deseeded and diced
- 1 courgette, diced
- 1 large beef tomato, diced
- sea salt and freshly ground black pepper
- handful of coriander leaves, to garnish

1 Place the farro in a large, lidded saucepan and cover with water. Place over a medium heat, cover, and simmer for about 1 hour or until almost all the water has been absorbed. Drain any remaining water and set aside.

2 Place a large, lidded saucepan over a medium heat. Add the coconut milk, stock, tomato purée, Thai red curry paste, and sugar and stir to combine. Cover and bring to the boil, stirring occasionally to make sure the ingredients are well combined. Then reduce the heat to a low simmer and cook the soup for a further 20 minutes.

3 Meanwhile, heat the oil in a large frying pan over a medium heat. Add the leeks and green peppers and sauté for 10 minutes or until softened and browned in places. Add the courgette and cook for a further 3 minutes. Remove from the heat and set aside.

4 Add the tomatoes to the soup. Taste and adjust the seasoning and cook the soup, stirring once, for 5 minutes. Then add the leek mixture and the farro. Stir well to mix and remove from the heat. Ladle the soup into bowls and garnish with coriander. Serve hot with a green salad and crusty ciabatta bread.

CHICKPEA, GARLIC, AND SPELT SOUP

This healthy and simple soup contains just the right balance of texture, from the chickpeas and spelt, and flavour, from the fresh herbs and chilli flakes. Serve it with some crusty wholegrain bread for a satisfying meal.

SERVES 4 · PREP 15 MINS, PLUS OVERNIGHT SOAKING · COOK 1 HR 20 MINS

120g (4¼oz) uncooked spelt

salt and freshly ground black pepper

2 tbsp extra virgin olive oil

1 onion, finely chopped

1 tsp finely chopped rosemary

1 tsp finely chopped thyme

5 garlic cloves, crushed and sliced

a pinch or two of chilli flakes

400g can chickpeas, drained

8–10 kale leaves, stalks removed and finely chopped

2 tbsp lemon juice

1.2 litres (2 pints) vegetable or chicken stock

1 tbsp freshly grated Parmesan cheese, to serve

1 Place the spelt in a bowl, cover with water, and leave to soak overnight. Then drain, rinse under running water, and place in a saucepan. Cover with 750ml (1¼ pints) of water, add a pinch of salt, and bring to the boil. Then reduce the heat to a simmer, cover, and cook for about 50 minutes, until almost all the water has been absorbed. Remove from the heat and drain any remaining water. Cover and set aside.

2 Heat the oil in a large, heavy-based pot over a medium heat. Add the onions and cook for 2–3 minutes, stirring frequently, until softened. Then add the rosemary, thyme, garlic, and chilli flakes. Season with ½ teaspoon of salt and a good grinding of pepper. Cook, stirring, for about 2 minutes.

3 Add the chickpeas, kale, and lemon juice to the pot. Stir to combine and cook until the kale has just started to wilt. Add the stock and bring to the boil. Then reduce the heat to a simmer and cook for about 15 minutes. Add the spelt and cook for a further 5 minutes, stirring frequently. Remove from the heat, sprinkle with Parmesan, and serve warm.

thyme

LIGHT ASIAN COCONUT BROTH WITH CHICKEN AND MILLET

This light soup contains many ingredients that are popular in Asian cuisine. It is given an extra boost by the use of coconut oil, which contains nutrients to protect the heart and improve the immune system.

SERVES 2 · PREP 10 MINS · COOK 40 MINS

2 tbsp coconut oil

2 chicken thighs, cut into cubes

5cm (2in) piece of fresh ginger root, finely chopped

1 garlic clove, finely chopped

½ red chilli, deseeded and finely chopped

200ml (7fl oz) coconut milk

500ml (16fl oz) chicken stock

100g (3½oz) uncooked millet

200g (7oz) beansprouts

1 tbsp soy sauce

2 tbsp chopped coriander leaves, to garnish

1 Heat the oil in a large saucepan over a medium-high heat. Add the chicken to the pan and cook for about 5 minutes, stirring frequently, until evenly coloured all over.

2 Add the ginger, garlic, and chilli and cook for 2 minutes, stirring frequently. Then stir in the coconut milk, stock, and millet. Reduce the heat to a simmer and cook for about 15–20 minutes.

3 Add the beansprouts to the pan and cook for 10 minutes, until the millet is fluffy and the chicken has cooked through. Then stir in the soy sauce. Divide the broth equally between two soup bowls and garnish with the coriander. Serve hot.

coriander

WARM
AND COOL
SALADS

NUTTY BARLEY AND LENTIL SALAD

This is no boring salad! The combination of hearty barley and nutty, crunchy almonds and walnuts is well balanced by the contrasting tastes and textures of sweet, dried cranberries and salty goat's cheese.

SERVES 4 · PREP 10 MINS, PLUS OVERNIGHT SOAKING AND COOLING · COOK 30 MINS

75g (2½oz) uncooked pearl barley

400g can green lentils, drained

25g (scant 1oz) almonds, roughly chopped

25g (scant 1oz) walnuts, roughly chopped

50g (1¾oz) dried cranberries

100g (3½oz) soft goat's cheese, crumbled

100g (3½oz) rocket

1 Place the barley in a bowl, cover with water, and leave to soak overnight or for at least 8 hours. Then drain, rinse under running water, and drain well again.

2 Place the barley in a lidded saucepan and cover with plenty of water. Bring to the boil, then reduce the heat to a simmer, and cover. Cook for about 30 minutes or until the barley is tender. Remove from the heat, drain any remaining water, and leave to cool completely.

3 Once cooled, place the barley and lentils in a large bowl and mix lightly to combine. Add the almonds, walnuts, and cranberries and mix to combine. Sprinkle over the goat's cheese, add the rocket, and toss lightly. Divide the salad equally between four plates and serve immediately.

GRAIN EXCHANGE

Use the same amount of **wheat berries** in place of the barley and see p16–17 for advice on cooking times.

why not try..

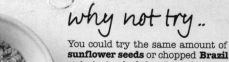

You could try the same amount of **sunflower seeds** or chopped **Brazil nuts** instead of the almonds or walnuts. You could also replace the rocket with the same quantity of **flat-leaf parsley**.

RAiNBOW WHEAT BERRY AND FETA CHEESE SALAD

This healthy salad is bursting with flavours and textures that bring together the nuttiness of the chewy wheat berries, the rich and soft feta, and the sweet and crunchy pomegranate seeds.

SERVES 2 · PREP 20 MiNS, PLUS OVERNiGHT SOAKiNG AND COOLiNG · COOK 30 MiNS

35g (1¼oz) uncooked wheat berries

1 carrot, grated

1 courgette, grated

50g (1¾oz) pumpkin seeds

100g (3½oz) feta cheese, crumbled

2 tbsp chopped flat-leaf parsley

seeds of 1 small pomegranate

salt and freshly ground black pepper

juice of 1 lemon (optional)

1 Place the wheat berries in a bowl, cover with water, and leave to soak overnight or for at least 8 hours. Then drain, rinse under running water, and drain well again.

2 Place the wheat berries in a lidded saucepan, cover with plenty of water, and bring to the boil, then reduce the heat to a simmer, and cover. Cook for 30 minutes, until the wheat berries are tender. Remove from the heat, drain any remaining water, and leave to cool completely.

3 Once cooled, place the wheat berries, carrots, and courgettes in a large bowl. Sprinkle over the pumpkin seeds and mix lightly to combine. Add the feta and parsley to the mixture and toss to combine.

4 Divide the salad equally between two salad bowls or plates. Sprinkle over the pomegranate seeds and season to taste. Drizzle with lemon juice, if using, and serve immediately.

GRAiN EXCHANGE

You could replace the wheat berries with the same quantity of one of the following grains.

farro

spelt

barley

why not try...

In place of the carrot, try adding a **finely chopped red pepper**. You could also replace the courgette with a quarter of **finely shredded red cabbage**.

MEDITERRANEAN TUNA AND FARRO SALAD

Farro makes a great substitute for rice and, with a traditional southern European medley of tomatoes, olives, and red onions, this lovely light salad is a great reminder of warm summer holidays.

SERVES 4 · PREP 15 MINS · COOK 30 MINS

100g (3½oz) uncooked farro

2 x 160g can tuna in spring water or brine, drained

5 sun-dried tomatoes in oil, roughly chopped

70g (2¼oz) green olives, pitted and halved

1 small red onion, diced

1 small red pepper, deseeded and cut into bite-sized pieces

1 small courgette, cut into bite-sized pieces

100g (3½oz) mixed salad leaves

4 tbsp chopped basil, to garnish

FOR THE DRESSING

3 tbsp extra virgin olive oil

2 tbsp balsamic vinegar

½ tsp Italian seasoning

1 garlic clove, crushed

salt and freshly ground black pepper

1 Place the farro in a large saucepan and cover with water. Bring to the boil, and then reduce the heat to a simmer. Cook for about 30 minutes or until tender. Remove from the heat, drain any remaining water, and leave to cool.

2 Use a fork to roughly flake the tuna from the cans and place in a large bowl. Add the tomatoes, olives, onions, red pepper, and courgette and mix well. Then add the cooled farro and mix until well combined.

3 For the dressing, place all the ingredients in a bowl and mix to combine. Taste and season with salt and pepper, if needed. Place the salad leaves on serving plates. Top with the tuna and farro mixture and pour over the dressing. Toss lightly to coat and garnish with basil. Serve immediately.

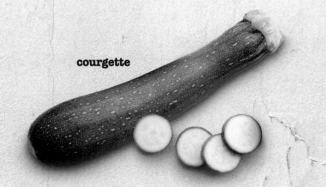

courgette

CHiCKEN AND PEANUT KAMUT SALAD

This nutty salad is a great way to use leftover chicken with a hint of lime for a zesty finish.

SERVES 2 · PREP 10 MiNS, PLUS SOAKiNG · COOK 45 MiNS

150g (5½oz) uncooked kamut

300g (10oz) cooked chicken breasts or thighs, shredded

4 spring onions, finely chopped

salt and freshly ground black pepper

20g (¾oz) salted peanuts

2 tbsp chopped coriander leaves, to garnish

FOR THE DRESSING

2 tbsp smooth peanut butter

juice of 1 lime

1 Place the kamut in a large bowl and cover with water. Leave to soak for 8 hours or for up to 24 hours. Then drain, rinse under running water, and drain well again.

2 Place the kamut in a large saucepan, cover with water, and bring to the boil. Then reduce the heat to a simmer and cook for 40–45 minutes. Remove from the heat and drain any remaining water. Set aside and keep warm.

3 For the dressing, place the peanut butter and lime juice in a small bowl. Add 2 tablespoons of water and whisk until well combined and thickened to the consistency of double cream.

4 Place the warm kamut in a large bowl. Add the chicken and onions and toss lightly to mix. Then pour the dressing over, season to taste, and mix well. Sprinkle over the peanuts, garnish with coriander, and serve immediately.

WARM HARiSSA, SORGHUM, AND CHiCKPEA SALAD

Harissa spices are combined with light and chewy sorghum for a Middle Eastern-inspired salad.

SERVES 4 · PREP 5 MiNS · COOK 1 HR

200g (7oz) uncooked sorghum

2 red peppers, deseeded and cut into bite-sized pieces

2 red onions, diced

1 tbsp light olive oil

2 x 400g can chickpeas, drained

1 tbsp harissa paste

juice of 1 lemon

salt and freshly ground black pepper

100g (3½oz) rocket leaves

4 tbsp roughly chopped flat-leaf parsley, to garnish

1 Rinse the sorghum under running water and place in a large, lidded saucepan. Cover with water and bring to the boil. Then reduce the heat to a simmer and cook, covered, for 50–60 minutes, until tender. Remove from the heat, drain any remaining water, and transfer to a large bowl.

2 Meanwhile, preheat the oven to 200°C (400°F/ Gas 6). Place the red peppers and onions in a baking tray. Drizzle over the oil and toss to coat. Bake in the oven for 30–40 minutes, until softened. Remove from the heat. Add the red peppers and onions to the sorghum and mix well.

3 Add the chickpeas and harissa paste to the sorghum mixture. Toss to combine, making sure the vegetables and chickpeas are evenly covered with the paste. Pour over the lemon juice and season to taste. Divide the rocket between four plates and top with the sorghum salad. Garnish with parsley and serve immediately.

MEXICAN QUINOA SALAD

Fresh vegetables, crunchy tortilla chips, and spicy chillies come together to create a dish that packs a real punch in flavour and texture. A salad that everyone can enjoy.

SERVES 2 · PREP 15 MINS, PLUS COOLING · COOK 20 MINS

50g (1¾oz) uncooked quinoa

400g can red kidney beans, drained

50g can sweetcorn

½ red onion, finely chopped

1 red pepper, deseeded and finely chopped

4–6 slices pickled jalapeño chillies, finely chopped

1 avocado, pitted and cut into cubes

1 head of romaine lettuce

50g (1¾oz) plain corn tortilla chips, crumbled, plus extra to serve

1 lemon or lime, halved, to serve

1 Rinse the quinoa under running water, drain, and place in a lidded saucepan. Cover with 250ml (9fl oz) of water and bring to the boil.

2 Reduce the heat to a simmer, cover, and cook for 15–20 minutes or until almost all the liquid has been absorbed and the quinoa is fluffy. Remove from the heat, drain any remaining water, and set aside to cool.

3 Place the quinoa, kidney beans, sweetcorn, onions, peppers, and jalapeños in a large bowl. Mix until well combined. Then add the avocado and mix lightly to combine.

4 Roughly shred the lettuce and add to the bowl. Sprinkle the tortillas over the mixture and toss lightly. Transfer the salad to a serving platter or plate. Serve immediately with tortilla chips and lemons or limes to squeeze over.

GRAIN EXCHANGE

Instead of the quinoa, use the same quantity of **millet**.

why not try...

Use a 400g can of **black beans**, drained, in place of the kidney beans.

AVOCADO, CORIANDER, AND LIME TABBOULEH

Tabbouleh is traditionally served as part of a mezze in the Middle East, but it also makes an excellent salad on its own or to accompany cold meats. The lime and avocado in this version give it a fresh dimension.

SERVES 4 · PREP 15 MINS, PLUS SOAKING AND CHILLING

175g (6oz) bulgur wheat

1½ tsp rock salt

2 tomatoes, diced

1 avocado, peeled, pitted, and diced

1 small red pepper, deseeded and diced

60g (2oz) red onion, diced

handful of coriander leaves, roughly chopped

125ml (4¼fl oz) lime juice

2 tbsp extra virgin olive oil

salt and freshly ground black pepper

1 Place 350ml (12fl oz) of water in a large saucepan and bring to the boil. Place the bulgur wheat and rock salt in a large bowl. Pour over the boiling water, cover, and leave to soak for about 30 minutes.

2 Drain any excess water from the bulgur wheat and place it in a large bowl. Then add the tomatoes, avocado, red peppers, onions, and coriander. Mix well to combine. Transfer the mixture to a large serving bowl.

3 Drizzle the lime juice and oil over the mixture. Toss well to coat. Season to taste with salt and black pepper, if needed. Mix well and chill the tabbouleh in the fridge for about 20 minutes before serving.

TOMATO, GOAT'S CHEESE, AND WATERMELON STACKS WITH TOASTED SPELT

The perfect healthy salad for a warm summer day, the contrasting textures and flavours, from the toasted spelt, creamy goat's cheese, and refreshing watermelon, make an excellent combination.

MAKES 4 STACKS · PREP 20 MINS, PLUS OVERNIGHT SOAKING · COOK 50 MINS

150g (5½oz) uncooked spelt, soaked

salt and freshly ground black pepper

1 tbsp olive oil

2 beef tomatoes, about 550g (1¼lb) in total, sliced into 8 rounds

225g (8oz) goat's cheese, sliced into thin rounds

1½kg (3lb 3oz) watermelon, deseeded and sliced into rounds

handful of basil leaves

a good drizzle of extra virgin olive oil

1 Place the spelt in a large bowl, cover with water, and leave to soak overnight or for about 8 hours. Then drain, rinse under running water, and drain well again.

2 Place the spelt in a lidded saucepan. Cover with 750ml (1¼ pints) of water, add a pinch of salt, and bring to the boil. Then reduce the heat to a simmer and cover. Cook for about 40 minutes, until all the water has been absorbed. Remove from the heat and drain the remaining water. Heat the olive oil in a large non-stick frying pan over a medium heat. Add the spelt and cook for about 10 minutes, stirring frequently, until golden brown. Remove from the heat and leave to cool.

3 To assemble the stacks, place a slice of tomato on each of four serving plates and season with salt and pepper. Top each one with a slice of cheese, a slice of watermelon, and a few basil leaves. Repeat to get one more layer of each, then sprinkle over a few spoonfuls of the toasted spelt. Drizzle over the extra virgin olive oil and season to taste if needed. Serve immediately.

watermelon

MEDITERRANEAN SALAD BOATS

The flavours of the Mediterranean come together in this quick and easy salad that is as colourful as it is satisfying.

SERVES 4 · PREP 15 MINS

1 large tomato, deseeded and diced

1 cucumber, diced

1 red pepper, deseeded and diced

70g (2¼oz) kalamata olives, pitted and halved

115g (4oz) feta cheese, crumbled

200g (7oz) prepared quinoa (see p22)

2 tbsp extra virgin olive oil

2 tbsp lemon juice

1 garlic clove, crushed

1 tbsp chopped oregano

salt and freshly ground black pepper

1 romaine heart, leaves separated

1 Place the tomatoes, cucumber, red pepper, olives, feta, and quinoa in a large bowl and toss to combine. Place the oil, lemon juice, garlic, and oregano in a separate bowl. Whisk to combine.

2 Pour the oil mixture over the salad and toss to coat. Season to taste with salt and pepper and divide the salad between four serving plates. Top with equal quantities of the romaine leaves and serve immediately.

STRAWBERRY, FETA, AND WHEAT BERRY SALAD

Sweet strawberries pair perfectly with wheat berries and salty feta cheese in this cooling and fruity salad.

SERVES 2 · PREP 10 MINS, PLUS OVERNIGHT SOAKING AND COOLING · COOK 30 MINS

100g (3½oz) uncooked wheat berries

1 tbsp balsamic vinegar

3 tbsp extra virgin olive oil

salt and freshly ground black pepper

40g (1½oz) baby spinach

100g (3½oz) strawberries, trimmed and cut into bite-sized pieces

10g (¼oz) basil leaves, finely chopped

60g (2oz) feta cheese, crumbled

1 Place the wheat berries in a large bowl and cover with water. Leave to soak overnight or for about 8 hours. Then drain, rinse under running water, and drain well again.

2 Place the wheat berries in a large, lidded saucepan, cover with water, and bring to the boil. Then reduce the heat to a simmer, cover, and cook for about 30 minutes or until tender but chewy. Remove from the heat and discard any remaining water. Transfer to a large bowl and leave to cool for at least 10 minutes.

3 Meanwhile, place the balsamic vinegar and oil in a small bowl and mix until well combined. Season to taste and mix well. Add the spinach, strawberries, and basil to the wheat berries and mix well. Then add the feta and pour over the dressing. Toss to coat, making sure the feta is evenly distributed. Serve immediately.

WARM ROASTED BUTTERNUT SQUASH AND WHEAT BERRY SALAD

A great dish for cool, autumn days, this tangy salad is an excellent combination of sweet, roasted butternut squash and chewy wheat berries that are given an added salty element from the blue cheese.

SERVES 4 · PREP 15 MINS, PLUS OVERNIGHT SOAKING AND COOLING · COOK 1 HR

300g (10oz) uncooked wheat berries

2 tbsp olive oil, plus extra for greasing

800g (1¾lb) butternut squash, deseeded and cut into cubes

salt and freshly ground black pepper

150g (5½oz) blue cheese, such as Danish Blue, crumbled

125ml (4fl oz) balsamic vinegar

1 Place the wheat berries in a large bowl, cover with water, and leave to soak overnight or for about 8 hours. Then drain, rinse under running water, and drain well again.

2 Place the wheat berries in a large, lidded saucepan and cover with 900ml (1½ pints) of water. Bring to the boil, and then reduce the heat to a medium-low, cover, and simmer for about 50 minutes. Remove from the heat, drain any remaining water, and leave to cool slightly.

3 Meanwhile, preheat the oven to 200°C (400°F/Gas 6). Grease a baking tray with a little oil. Spread out the butternut squash on the tray in an even layer and drizzle over the oil. Season to taste and roast in the oven for 20 minutes. Then remove from the heat, stir to mix, and return to the oven. Roast for a further 20 minutes.

4 Place the wheat berries, butternut squash, and cheese in a large bowl and toss to combine. Drizzle over the balsamic vinegar and toss to coat. Taste and adjust the seasoning, if needed, and serve immediately.

butternut squash

GRiLLED BROCCOLi RABE AND BARLEY
WiTH A ROMESCO SAUCE

A tasty vegetarian recipe, this dish can be served as a filling main meal or even an impressive side. The flavour of the broccoli is enhanced by grilling and is well paired with the spicy Spanish sauce and fluffy barley.

SERVES 6-8 · PREP 10 MiNS, PLUS SOAKiNG · COOK 1 HR 5 MiNS

200g (7oz) uncooked barley

salt and freshly ground black pepper

600g (1lb 5oz) broccoli rabe

2 tbsp extra virgin olive oil

juice of ½ lemon

FOR THE SAUCE

25g (scant 1oz) dried ancho chillies, deseeded

50g (1¾oz) almonds, sliced

100g (3½oz) roasted red peppers from a jar

400g can chopped tomatoes

2 tbsp sherry vinegar

2 tbsp extra virgin olive oil

pinch of smoked paprika

1 Place the barley in a large saucepan and cover with 750ml (1¼ pints) of water. Add a pinch of salt and bring to the boil. Then reduce the heat to a simmer, cover, and cook for about 50 minutes or until almost all the water has been absorbed. Remove from the heat. Cover and set aside.

2 Meanwhile, for the sauce, place the ancho chillies in a small bowl, cover with water, and leave to soak for 10 minutes. Then drain the chillies and discard the water. Dice the chillies and set them aside. Place the almonds in a non-stick frying pan over a medium-low heat. Toast the almonds for 3–4 minutes or until lightly browned. Transfer the almonds to a food processor and pulse until they form a coarse flour.

3 Add the ancho chillies, roasted red peppers, tomatoes, sherry vinegar, oil, and smoked paprika to the food processor. Season with ¼ teaspoon of salt and a good grinding of pepper. Pulse until the mixture is smooth, but retains a little texture. Transfer the sauce to a bowl and set aside.

4 Place the broccoli in a large bowl. Drizzle over the oil, season to taste, and toss to coat. Heat a griddle pan over a medium-high heat. Grill the broccoli for 3–5 minutes on each side, until tender and starting to brown.

5 Remove the broccoli from the heat and drizzle over the lemon juice. On a large serving dish, spread out the barley and top with the broccoli. Pour over the desired quantity of romesco sauce. Serve immediately with the remaining sauce on the side.

CAPRESE FARRO SALAD

Featuring fresh summer tomatoes, soft mozzarella, chewy farro, and a homemade pesto sauce, this colourful and light italian salad makes the perfect starter for any meal.

SERVES 4 · PREP 10 MiNS, PLUS COOLING · COOK 50 MiNS

200g (7oz) uncooked farro

225g (8oz) mozzarella, diced

3 large tomatoes, cut into bite-sized pieces

FOR THE PESTO

45g (1½oz) basil leaves, rinsed and dried, plus extra to garnish

2 tbsp pine nuts

1 garlic clove

2–3 tbsp extra virgin olive oil

salt

1 Rinse the farro under cold running water and place in a large saucepan. Cover with about 600ml (1 pint) of water and bring to the boil. Then reduce the heat to a simmer and cook, stirring occasionally, for about 40 minutes or until softened. Remove from the heat, drain, and set aside to cool.

2 For the pesto, place the basil leaves, pine nuts, garlic, and oil in a food processor and pulse until smooth. Season to taste, if needed.

3 Place the mozzarella and tomatoes in a large bowl. Add the pesto and cooled farro and stir to mix. Chill the salad in the fridge until ready to serve, garnished with a few basil leaves.

GRAiN EXCHANGE

For a change, try using the same amount of **pearl barley** in place of the farro.

why not try...

You could replace the fresh mozzarella cheese with the same quantity of **burrata** cheese.

MiLLET, CORN, AND RED PEPPER SALAD
WiTH ROASTED LEEKS

Serving this light and healthy salad over leeks gives it a wonderful twist. The addition of yogurt provides the dish with a rich and creamy texture that is well balanced with the crunchiness of the peppers.

SERVES 6 · PREP 15 MiNS, PLUS SOAKiNG AND COOLING · COOK 40 MiNS

4 tbsp olive oil

100g (3½oz) uncooked millet

salt and freshly ground black pepper

1 small red onion, diced

2 red peppers, deseeded and diced

1 jalapeño, diced

½ tbsp cayenne pepper

4 whole corn on the cob, kernels removed

2 large poblano chillies, roasted, peeled, deseeded, and sliced into small strips

½ tsp smoked paprika

3 spring onions, thinly sliced

115g (4oz) plain yogurt

juice of 1 lime

6 leeks, bottoms and rough green tops trimmed, cleaned, and halved lengthways

1 Heat 1 tablespoon of the oil in a large, lidded saucepan over a medium heat. Add the millet and cook for 2–3 minutes, stirring frequently. Add ¼ teaspoon of salt, cover with 500ml (16fl oz) of water, and bring to the boil. Reduce the heat to a simmer, cover, and cook for 15 minutes. Remove from the heat. Leave to soak, covered, for about 10 minutes, then use a fork to fluff up the grain. Leave to cool.

2 Meanwhile, heat 1 tablespoon of the oil in a frying pan over a medium heat. Add the onions and red peppers and season well. Cook for 5 minutes, stirring, until the onions are translucent. Then add the jalapeños, cayenne pepper, corn, chillies, and smoked paprika. Cook for a further 5–10 minutes, stirring occasionally, until the corn is tender.

3 Reduce the heat to low and add the spring onions and yogurt. Cook for about 2 minutes, stirring, until the yogurt has melted. Then add the lime juice and season to taste. Transfer the mixture to a large bowl, add the cooled millet, and mix to combine. Set aside.

4 Set the grill at its medium setting. Brush the leeks with the remaining oil and season well. Grill the leeks for 20 minutes, turning over frequently, until tender and cooked through. Then transfer to a plate, cover with foil, and leave to steam for 5 minutes. Place the leeks on serving plates and spoon over the corn and millet salad. Serve warm.

CHICKEN CAESAR SALAD WITH POLENTA CROUTONS

This perennially popular salad is given a twist with the use of baked polenta to make crunchy croutons that provide extra texture to complement the succulence of the chicken and the freshness of the lettuce.

SERVES 4 · PREP 20 MINS · COOK 10 MINS

2 tbsp light olive oil

225g (8oz) prepared polenta (see p25), cut into 2.5cm (1in) cubes

rock salt and freshly ground black pepper

1 large or 2 small heads romaine lettuce, washed, dried, and torn into bite-sized pieces

225g (8oz) cooked chicken, cut into bite-sized pieces

85g (3oz) freshly grated Romano cheese

FOR THE DRESSING

100ml (3½fl oz) extra virgin olive oil

1 tbsp Dijon mustard

3 tbsp good-quality mayonnaise

4 anchovy fillets, chopped

½ tsp Worcestershire sauce

1 garlic clove, crushed

2 tbsp finely grated Parmesan cheese, plus extra to serve

pinch of caster sugar

1 Heat the oil in a large frying pan over a medium heat. Add the polenta and season with ½ teaspoon of rock salt and ¼ teaspoon of pepper. Cook for 10 minutes, turning over the polenta cubes occasionally, until lightly browned and crisp. Remove from the heat and set aside.

2 For the dressing, place all the ingredients in the small bowl of a food processor and pulse until emulsified into a thick and creamy dressing. Alternatively, place the ingredients in a large bowl and blend well with a hand-held blender. Season with pepper, mix well to combine, and set aside.

3 Place the lettuce, chicken, and cheese in a large bowl and toss lightly to combine. Drizzle over the dressing, a little at a time, and toss until well coated. Arrange the salad on a serving dish and scatter over the polenta croutons. Sprinkle over some Parmesan and serve immediately.

CARAMELIZED ONiON AND KALE WHEAT BERRY SALAD WiTH GRiLLED STEAK

A great meal to enjoy al fresco, sweet caramelized onions and earthy kale are combined with nutty wheat berries in this crunchy summer salad. if preferred, you can use a different cut of steak, such as rump or fillet.

SERVES 4 · PREP 10 MiNS, PLUS OVERNiGHT SOAKiNG AND RESTiNG · COOK 1 HR 20 MiNS

300g (10oz) wheat berries, soaked overnight

450g (1lb) sirloin steak

salt and freshly ground black pepper

2 tbsp olive oil

2 onions, halved and thinly sliced

100g (3½oz) kale, roughly chopped

60ml (2fl oz) balsamic vinegar

1 Place the wheat berries in a lidded saucepan and cover with 900ml (1½ pints) of water. Bring to the boil, then reduce the heat to medium-low, and cover. Cook for about 50 minutes or until all the water has been absorbed. Remove from the heat, drain any remaining water, and place in a large bowl. Set aside.

2 Set the grill at its medium setting and season the steak on both sides. Grill the steak for 6–8 minutes on each side, or until cooked to the desired doneness. Remove from the heat and leave to rest and cool for at least 10 minutes. Then slice the steak into thin strips and set aside.

3 Meanwhile, heat the oil in a large frying pan over a medium heat. Add the onions and season well. Cook, stirring frequently, for 10–15 minutes, until softened and golden brown. Then add the kale and vinegar, cover, and cook for about 5 minutes or until the kale has softened slightly. Remove from the heat.

5 Add the onion and kale mixture to the wheat berries and toss well to combine. Divide the salad evenly between four plates and top with the sliced steak. Serve immediately.

kale

CHOPPED KALE, FREEKEH, COURGETTE, AND CORN SALAD
WITH GARLIC TAHINI

Chopped salads are easy to throw together and a great way to use up surplus ingredients in the fridge. Beautifully summery, this salad is best served when courgettes and sweetcorn are in their peak season.

SERVES 4–6 · PREP 20 MINS, PLUS COOLING · COOK 30 MINS

175g (6oz) uncooked freekeh

600ml (1 pint) vegetable stock

2 corn on the cob

1 tbsp olive oil

75g (2½oz) almonds, roughly chopped

30g (1oz) sesame seeds

10–12 kale leaves, ribs removed and finely chopped

425g can chopped chickpeas

4–6 spring onions, chopped

1 green courgette, diced

1 yellow courgette, diced

FOR THE DRESSING

3 tbsp tahini

1 garlic clove, pressed

2 tbsp lemon juice

1 tsp low-sodium soy sauce

1 tsp toasted sesame oil

salt and freshly ground black pepper

1 Rinse the freekeh under cold running water, drain well, and place in a lidded saucepan. Add the stock and bring to the boil. Then reduce the heat to a simmer, cover, and cook for about 20 minutes. Remove from the heat and leave to stand, covered, for 5 minutes. Then uncover and leave to cool completely.

2 Bring a large pan of water to the boil. Add the corn and cook for 10 minutes or until the corn kernels are tender. Remove from the pan and rinse under cold running water. Remove the kernels from the cob by slicing down lengthways with a knife.

3 For the dressing, place the tahini, garlic, lemon juice, soy sauce, and sesame oil in a small bowl. Add 2 tablespoons of water, and whisk until well combined. Taste, adjusting the seasoning if necessary, and set aside.

4 Heat the olive oil in a small non-stick frying pan over a low heat. Add the almonds and sesame seeds and toast for 2–3 minutes or until the almonds are lightly browned. Remove from the heat and leave to cool.

5 Place the kale in a large bowl and drizzle with some of the dressing. Toss well to coat. Then add the corn, almonds, sesame seeds, chickpeas, spring onions, and green and yellow courgettes. Drizzle over more of the seasoning and toss well to coat. Add the freekeh and the remaining seasoning and mix well to combine. Serve immediately.

QUINOA AND FENNEL SALAD

The peppery and aniseed notes of fennel are combined with spring onions and coriander in this salad. They contrast well with the nuttiness of the quinoa and the juicy and sweet pomegranate seeds.

SERVES 4 · PREP 10 MINS, PLUS STANDING · COOK 15 MINS

175g (6oz) uncooked quinoa

350ml (12fl oz) vegetable stock

1 tsp ground cumin

1 whole fennel bulb

3 tbsp olive oil

1 tbsp lemon juice

salt and freshly ground black pepper

4 spring onions, trimmed and thinly sliced

3 tbsp chopped coriander leaves

2 tbsp chopped mint leaves

100g (3½oz) pomegranate seeds

1 Rinse the quinoa under cold running water. Drain and place in a large saucepan. Add the stock and cumin and bring to the boil, stirring frequently. Then cover and cook over a medium heat for about 10 minutes. Remove from the heat and drain. Return the quinoa to the pan and leave for about 10 minutes, covered, to fluff up.

2 To prepare the fennel, trim the stalks, root end, and any tough outer pieces from the bulb and reserve the fronds. Cut the bulb in half lengthways. Then set each half on a chopping board, flat-side down, and cut into thin slices lengthways.

3 Heat 2 tablespoons of the oil in a large frying pan over a medium heat. Add the fennel slices and cook for about 5 minutes, turning over once, until golden. Remove from the heat and transfer to a bowl. Add the lemon juice and remaining oil, season to taste, and mix well to combine.

4 Add the onions, coriander, mint, and reserved fennel fronds to the bowl. Then add the quinoa and half the pomegranate seeds. Stir to mix, taste, and adjust the seasoning if needed. Divide the salad between four plates and sprinkle over the remaining pomegranate seeds. Serve at room temperature or cold.

FREEKEH SWEET AND SPICY WARM SALAD

This warming and colourful salad combines sweet roasted squash and sticky dates with a fragrant and spiced freekeh and is perfect for autumn and winter lunches.

SERVES 4 · PREP 15 MINS, PLUS COOLING · COOK 40 MINS

2 tsp ground cinnamon

1 tsp grated ginger

1 tsp ground cumin

2 tbsp light olive oil

1 butternut squash, deseeded and cut into 2cm (¾in) cubes

200g (7oz) cracked freekeh

1 small head radicchio, roughly chopped

8 dried pitted dates, about 40g (1½oz) in total, roughly chopped

4 tbsp roughly chopped flat-leaf parsley

FOR THE DRESSING

4 tbsp extra virgin olive oil

juice of 1 lemon

1 tbsp honey

salt and freshly ground black pepper

1 Preheat the oven to 200°C (400°F/Gas 6). Place the cinnamon, ginger, cumin, and oil in a small bowl and mix to combine. Place the butternut squash in a baking tray, pour the mixture over, and toss to coat. Bake in the oven for 30–35 minutes or until the squash is tender.

2 Meanwhile, rinse the freekeh under running water and place in a large saucepan. Cover with 1 litre (1¾ pints) of water and bring to the boil. Then reduce the heat to a simmer and cook for 15 minutes or until almost all the water has been absorbed. Remove from the heat, drain any remaining water, and leave to cool slightly.

3 For the dressing, place all the ingredients in a bowl. Season to taste and mix to combine. Place the radicchio and dates in a large serving dish. Add the squash and freekeh and toss lightly to mix. Then pour over the dressing, season to taste, and toss until well combined. Serve warm garnished with parsley.

GRAIN EXCHANGE

This dish works well with a variety of similar grains. Try replacing the freekeh with the same amount of the following grains and see p16–17 for advice on cooking times.

quinoa

farro

millet

why not try...

Try using 2 large **sweet potatoes** in place of the squash, and cook in the same way. You can also use **chicory** or **rocket leaves** instead of the radicchio.

BRiGHT STiR-FRiES

CHINESE 5-SPICE PORK WITH MILLET

This easy-to-make stir-fry brings together tender pork, light and fresh greens, and chewy millet. Sweet and spicy, it's perfect for a quick yet flavour-packed lunch or dinner.

SERVES 4 · PREP 10 MINS, PLUS MARINATING · COOK 40 MINS

4 tbsp honey

6 tbsp soy sauce

2 tbsp Chinese 5-spice powder

450g (1lb) pork tenderloin, cut into bite-sized pieces

200g (7oz) uncooked millet

2 tbsp light olive oil

300g (10oz) spring greens, cores removed and cut into ribbons

200g (7oz) pak choi, cores removed and cut into ribbons

1 Place the honey, soy sauce, and 5-spice powder in a bowl and mix to combine. Add the pork and mix until well coated. Cover the bowl with a kitchen towel and place in the fridge. Leave to marinate for at least 2 hours or up to 24 hours.

2 Place the millet and 125ml (4¼fl oz) water in a large saucepan and bring to the boil. Then reduce the heat to a simmer and cook for about 15 minutes or until all the water has been absorbed and the millet is cooked through. Remove from the heat and set aside.

3 Heat the oil in a large saucepan over a medium-high heat. Add the pork and marinade to the pan and cook, stirring occasionally, for about 10 minutes or until the pork is cooked through. Do this in batches to avoid overcrowding the pan. Remove with a slotted spoon and set aside.

4 Increase the heat to high and add 65ml (2¼fl oz) of water to the pan. Stir to mix with any marinade left in the pan and bring to the boil. Then add the spring greens and pak choi and cook for 3–4 minutes, until tender. Return the pork to the pan and stir in the millet. Stir well to combine and remove from the heat. Serve hot.

GRAIN EXCHANGE

Try using one of the following grains in place of the millet. use the same amount of the quinoa, as given for the millet and cook as instructed. For the kamut, use 150g (5½oz) of grain and see p16 for advice on additional cooking time.

quinoa

kamut

why not try...

In place of spring greens, try adding the same amount of **broccoli** or **kale**.

THAI PEANUT AND WHEAT BERRY STIR-FRY

Peanut butter works well with rich soy beans and wheat berries to create a light, yet filling, stir-fry.

SERVES 2 · PREP 10 MINS, PLUS OVERNIGHT SOAKING
COOK 1 HR

100g (3½oz) uncooked wheat berries	50g (1¾oz) green cabbage, shredded
2 tbsp smooth peanut butter	1 carrot, sliced into matchsticks
2 tbsp honey	100g (3½oz) soya beans
1 tbsp soy sauce	salt and freshly ground black pepper
¼ tsp chilli flakes	
juice of 1 lime	2 tbsp roughly chopped coriander leaves
1 tbsp vegetable oil	
75g (2½oz) bean sprouts	

1 Place the wheat berries in a bowl and cover with water. Leave to soak for 8 hours or up to 24 hours. Then drain, rinse under running water, and drain again. Place in a pan, cover with water, and bring to the boil. Then reduce the heat to a simmer, cover, and cook for 40–45 minutes, until tender. Remove from the heat and drain any remaining water.

2 Place the peanut butter, honey, soy sauce, and chilli flakes in a bowl and mix to combine. Then add the lime juice and mix until it forms a smooth sauce. Heat the oil in a large frying pan over a high heat. Add the bean sprouts, cabbage, and carrots and stir-fry for 3–5 minutes. Then add the soya beans and wheat berries and stir-fry for a further 2 minutes. Pour over the peanut sauce and toss to coat. Season to taste and remove from the heat. Sprinkle with coriander and serve hot.

GARLIC AND GINGER BEEF WITH GREENS AND SPELT

Spring greens make a tasty alternative to pak choi in this classic beef and ginger combination.

SERVES 2 · PREP 15 MINS, PLUS OVERNIGHT SOAKING
COOK 45 MINS

100g (3½oz) uncooked spelt, soaked overnight	300g (10oz) beef featherblade steak, cut into strips
2 tbsp light olive oil	1 tbsp honey
5cm (2in) piece of fresh root ginger, grated	1 tbsp soy sauce, plus extra if needed
3 garlic cloves, crushed	100g (3½oz) spring greens, shredded

1 Rinse the spelt under running water, drain well, and place in a large, lidded saucepan. Cover with water and bring to the boil. Then reduce the heat to a simmer, cover, and cook for 40 minutes.

2 Heat the oil in a large frying pan over a medium heat. Add the ginger and garlic and sauté for about 5 minutes. Increase the heat to medium-high, add the beef, and cook for 3 minutes. Then add the honey and soy sauce, mix well, and increase the heat to high. Cook, stirring frequently, for 2 minutes or until the liquid is reduced to a thick sauce.

3 Reduce the heat to medium. Add the spring greens and toss lightly to combine. Then add the spelt and mix well. Cook for 3–4 minutes, stirring, until the spring greens are lightly cooked. Taste, and add more soy sauce if needed. Remove from the heat and serve hot.

AUBERGINE, COURGETTE, KALE, AND BUCKWHEAT STIR-FRY
WITH A GINGER MISO

This delicious and colourful dish includes a variety of vegetables, as well as hearty and filling buckwheat, and can be served as a starter or even a main meal. Try to use the traditional Japanese aubergines because they are sweeter than regular ones.

SERVES 4 · PREP 15 MINS · COOK 15 MINS

sea salt

175g (6oz) uncooked buckwheat

3 tbsp grapeseed oil

2 dried red chillies

1 garlic clove, thinly sliced

1 tsp grated fresh root ginger

drizzle of toasted sesame oil (optional)

4 Japanese aubergines, cut into cubes

2 courgettes, cut into cubes

4 kale leaves, ribs removed and roughly chopped

handful of basil leaves, roughly chopped

sesame seeds, to garnish

FOR THE MISO

2 tbsp white miso

1½ tsp brown rice vinegar

1 tsp grated fresh root ginger

1 Place 500ml (16fl oz) of water in a large, lidded saucepan and add a pinch of salt. Bring to the boil, then slowly stir in the buckwheat. Reduce the heat to a simmer, cover, and cook for 15 minutes. Then remove from the heat, cover, and leave to stand.

2 Meanwhile, heat the grapeseed oil in a large frying pan over a medium heat. Add the chillies and cook for about 2 minutes, stirring, until fragrant. Add the garlic, ginger, and sesame oil, if using, and cook for 2 minutes, stirring frequently. Then add the aubergines and courgettes and cook for a further 8–10 minutes, stirring frequently, until the vegetables are cooked through.

3 Meanwhile, for the miso, place all the ingredients in a bowl, add 1 teaspoon of water, and mix until well combined. Stir the mixture into the vegetables and mix well to coat. Then add the kale and cook for a further 2–3 minutes, until just wilted. Remove from the heat and sprinkle over the basil and sesame seeds. Serve hot over the buckwheat.

dried red chillies

SWEET AND SPiCY SALMON AND QUiNOA STiR-FRY

Tender salmon fillets, marinated in a sweet orange juice and honey mixture, are beautifully paired with a rich and spicy stir-fry sauce, nutty quinoa, and fresh greens to make a flavour-packed and filling supper.

SERVES 2 · PREP 10 MiNS, PLUS COOLING AND MARiNATiNG · COOK 40 MiNS

2 salmon fillets, about 150g (5½oz) each

100g (3½oz) uncooked quinoa

1 tbsp light olive oil

1 head of pak choi, white core removed and leaves sliced into ribbons

200g (7oz) beansprouts

FOR THE MARiNADE

200ml (7fl oz) orange juice

4 tbsp honey

½ tsp dried chilli flakes

1 tbsp soy sauce

1 For the marinade, place all the ingredients in a large saucepan and bring to the boil over a medium-high heat. Then reduce the heat to a simmer and cook for about 8–10 minutes until the liquid has reduced. Remove from the heat and leave to cool.

2 Place the salmon in a large plastic bag and pour the marinade over. Seal the bag, place in the fridge, and leave to marinate for about 2 hours or overnight.

3 Preheat the oven to 200°C (400°F/Gas 6). Remove the salmon from the bag and place each one in the middle of a square sheet of foil. Roll up the sides to make baskets and pour over any remaining marinade. Continue to roll up the sides to seal the parcels and place them on a baking tray. Bake for about 20 minutes or until the salmon is cooked.

4 Meanwhile, rinse the quinoa under running water and place in a large saucepan. Add 250ml (9fl oz) of water and bring to a simmer over a medium heat. Cook for about 15 minutes or until all the liquid has been absorbed and the grain is fluffy.

5 Heat the oil in a large frying pan over a high heat. Add the pak choi and beansprouts and fry for 3–4 minutes. Then add the cooked quinoa, mix well, and remove from the heat. Divide the quinoa and vegetable mixture between two plates. Place the salmon steaks on top and pour over any remaining juices from the foil parcels. Serve hot.

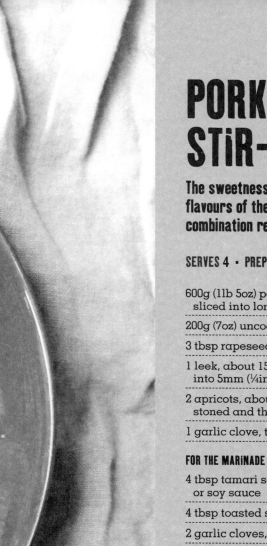

PORK, APRICOT, AND LEEK STIR-FRY WITH FREEKEH

The sweetness of the apricot in this dish complements the rich and savoury flavours of the freekeh and tamari sauce. Pairing the pork with this tantalising combination results in a truly satisfying meal.

SERVES 4 · PREP 15 MINS, PLUS MARINATING · COOK 1 HR 10 MINS

600g (1lb 5oz) pork shoulder, sliced into long, thin pieces

200g (7oz) uncooked freekeh

3 tbsp rapeseed oil

1 leek, about 150g (5½oz), cut into 5mm (¼in) rounds

2 apricots, about 140g (5oz), stoned and thinly sliced

1 garlic clove, thinly sliced

FOR THE MARINADE

4 tbsp tamari sauce or soy sauce

4 tbsp toasted sesame oil

2 garlic cloves, crushed

½ tsp sugar

1 For the marinade, place all the ingredients in a large bowl and whisk to combine. Add the pork and mix to coat. Transfer to the fridge and leave to marinate for 20–30 minutes.

2 Meanwhile, place the freekeh in a large, lidded saucepan. Pour over 1 litre (1¾ pints) of water and bring to the boil. Then reduce the heat to a simmer, cover, and cook for about 45 minutes or until chewy. Remove from the heat and drain any remaining water. Cover and set aside.

3 Heat 2 tablespoons of the oil in a large frying pan over a medium heat. Add the leeks and cook for about 5 minutes, stirring frequently, until softened. Remove with a slotted spoon, place on a plate, and set aside. Then add the apricots to the pan and sauté for about 2 minutes or until just starting to soften, but not brown. Remove from the pan and set aside with the leeks.

4 Pour the remaining oil into the pan, add the garlic, and cook for 1–2 minutes. Then add the pork and marinade and cook, stirring frequently, for about 5 minutes or until the pork just starts to brown. Return the leeks and apricots to the pan and cook, stirring frequently, for a further 5 minutes or until the pork is lightly browned all over and cooked through. Remove from the heat. Serve immediately, along with the freekeh.

MiLLET CASHEW STiR-FRY
WiTH CHiLLi AND LiME SAUCE

This simple stir-fry is light, yet full of flavour and colour. The lime gives it an added zing that pairs well with the sweetness of the toasted cashews and crunchy vegetables.

SERVES 2 · PREP 20 MiNS · COOK 20 MiNS

100g (3½oz) uncooked millet

50g (1¾oz) cashew nuts

2 tbsp light olive oil

115g (4oz) carrot, roughly chopped

115g (4oz) cabbage, roughly chopped

100g (3½oz) bean sprouts

85g (3oz) red onion, thinly sliced

FOR THE SAUCE

juice of 1 lime and grated zest of ½ lime

2 tbsp soy sauce

2 tbsp honey

1 red chilli, deseeded and finely chopped

1 Place the millet in a large saucepan. Cover with 125ml (4¼fl oz) of water and simmer for about 10 minutes or until all the water has been absorbed. Then remove from the heat and set aside.

2 Heat a large wok or frying pan over a high heat. Add the cashew nuts and toast until lightly coloured. Remove from the heat and roughly chop. Add the oil to the pan. Then add the carrots, cabbage, bean sprouts, and onions. Cook, stirring frequently, for about 5 minutes or until lightly cooked.

3 Meanwhile, for the sauce, place all the ingredients in a bowl and mix to combine. Add the millet to the vegetables and mix well. Pour over the chilli and lime sauce, mix well, and cook for 1–2 minutes. Remove from the heat and serve hot.

GRAiN EXCHANGE

For a variation, try replacing the millet with the same amount of quinoa. Or you could use 120g (4¼oz) of bulgur wheat and cook it in about 600ml (1 pint) of water.

quinoa

bulgur wheat

POBLANOS STUFFED WiTH SPiCY SORGHUM AND BLACK BEAN STiR-FRY

Green poblano peppers have a sweet and mild heat that makes them the perfect companion for this well-spiced sorghum stir-fry. An impressive dish, it's also easy to make.

SERVES 6 · PREP 10 MiNUTES, PLUS COOLING · COOK 1 HR 20 MiNUTES

100g (3½oz) uncooked sorghum

500ml (16fl oz) vegetable stock

6 large poblano peppers

2 tbsp sunflower oil

salt and freshly ground black pepper

1 small red onion, roughly chopped

3 garlic cloves, crushed

1 tsp chilli powder

1 tsp oregano

½ tsp ground cumin

¼ tsp cayenne pepper

400g can black beans, drained and rinsed

150g (5½oz) plum tomatoes, deseeded and diced

150g can corn kernels

1 tbsp freshly grated Cheddar cheese, to serve

1 Place the sorghum and stock in a small, lidded saucepan and bring to the boil. Then reduce to a simmer, cover, and cook for about 45 minutes. Remove from the heat and leave, covered, for a further 10 minutes. Then drain any remaining water and set aside.

2 Meanwhile, preheat the oven to 230°C (450°F/Gas 8). Place the poblano peppers on a lined baking sheet. Brush with half of the oil and season with salt and pepper. Place in the oven and roast for 15–20 minutes, until they start to brown and are tender. Remove from the heat and leave to cool slightly. Once cool enough to handle, slit the peppers in the centre, lengthways, and remove the seeds.

3 Heat the remaining oil in a large cast-iron pan over a medium heat. Add the onions and sauté for 5–8 minutes or until softened. Then add the garlic, chilli powder, oregano, cumin, and cayenne pepper. Mix to combine and cook for 2–3 minutes, stirring frequently.

4 Add the sorghum, beans, and tomatoes and stir to combine. Cook for 5 minutes, stirring occasionally. Then add the corn and cook for a further 2–3 minutes. Taste, and adjust the seasoning if needed. Spoon the stir-fry mixture into the poblano peppers and scatter any extra on the plates. Garnish with Cheddar and serve immediately.

SWEET AND SOUR CHICKEN WITH KAMUT

A different take on the popular sweet and sour chicken, this recipe adds kamut to the traditional Chinese dish for a nuttier flavour and a new wholesome texture.

SERVES 2–3 · PREP 15 MINS, PLUS OVERNIGHT SOAKING · COOK 55 MINS

100g (3½oz) uncooked kamut

2 tbsp cornflour

425g can pineapple chunks, natural juices reserved

2 tbsp rice wine vinegar

3 tbsp honey

2 tbsp tomato purée

2 tbsp soy sauce, plus extra if needed

1 tbsp sunflower oil

2 skinless chicken breasts, cut into bite-sized pieces

1 small onion, roughly chopped

1 red pepper, deseeded and cut into chunks

75g (2½oz) baby sweetcorn, cut into quarters

salt and freshly ground black pepper

1 Place the kamut in a large bowl and cover with water. Leave to soak for about 8 hours or for up to 24 hours. Drain any remaining water. Rinse under running water and drain well.

2 Place the kamut in a saucepan and cover with water. Bring to the boil, then reduce the heat to a simmer. Cover and cook for 40–45 minutes or until tender. Drain and set aside.

3 Meanwhile, mix the cornflour with 3 tablespoons of the pineapple juice in a small bowl. Then add the vinegar, honey, tomato purée, soy sauce, and remaining pineapple juice. Mix until well combined.

4 Heat the oil in a large frying pan over a medium-high heat. Add the chicken and cook for about 3 minutes, stirring frequently, until lightly coloured. Then add the onions, red peppers, and sweetcorn. Cook for 3 minutes, stirring frequently, until the onions are translucent.

5 Add the pineapple and cornflour mixture and bring to the boil. Then reduce the heat to a simmer and cook for 2–3 minutes, until the sauce has thickened and the chicken has cooked through. Taste, adjusting the seasoning, if needed, and add more soy sauce if required. Serve the kamut topped with the chicken and vegetables.

GRAIN EXCHANGE

This dish works really well with a variety of similar grains. For a variation, try replacing the kamut with the same amount of any of the following grains and see p16–17 for advice on cooking times.

spelt

barley

wheat berries

why not try...

Instead of chicken, you could use the same amount of **duck breast,** or one **skinless turkey breast,** or 225g (8oz) of **pork fillet.**

AMARANTH-CRUSTED TOFU
WiTH GREEN BEANS AND BLACK RiCE

This vegetarian dish uses coarse amaranth flour and sesame seeds in place of breadcrumbs to coat tender tofu, giving it a crunchy, nutty texture, and pairs it with a spicy, salty green bean stir-fry.

SERVES 4 · PREP 15 MiNS · COOK 50 MiNS

300g packet of black rice

400g (14oz) extra firm tofu, drained

4 tbsp amaranth flour

3 tbsp sesame seeds, plus extra to serve

1 egg, lightly beaten

salt and freshly ground black pepper

2–3 tbsp grapeseed oil

2 tbsp sesame oil, plus extra to serve

1 onion, thinly sliced

1 tsp grated fresh root ginger

3 mild red chillies, deseeded and sliced into 1cm (½in) pieces

3 garlic cloves, crushed and thinly sliced

200g (7oz) green beans, blanched

1 tbsp tamari sauce, plus extra to serve

2 spring onions, cut into 2.5cm (1in) long pieces

1 Place the rice in a large saucepan and cook according to packet instructions. Remove from the heat, cover, and set aside. Pat the tofu dry with kitchen paper and cut 16 x 2.5cm (1in) thick triangles. Set aside.

2 Place the amaranth flour and sesame seeds in a shallow dish and mix to combine. Place the egg in a small bowl. Season the tofu with salt and pepper and brush lightly with the egg. Then toss the tofu in the amaranth flour mixture until lightly coated.

3 Heat the grapeseed oil in a large frying pan over a medium-low heat. Once the oil has heated, reduce the heat to low and add the tofu. Cook for 3–4 minutes on each side, turning the tofu gently to prevent it breaking apart, until evenly browned on each side. Remove with a slotted spoon, set aside on a lined plate, and keep warm. Drain the excess oil from the pan.

4 Add the sesame oil to the pan and increase the heat to medium. Add the onions, ginger, and chillies. Cook for about 5 minutes, stirring frequently, until softened. Then add the garlic and cook for another minute. Add the green beans and cook, stirring, for 3–4 minutes.

5 Add the tamari sauce and spring onions. Season with pepper and cook, stirring, for about 3 minutes. Add the tofu and gently heat through for 2 minutes. Do not stir the tofu as it may break apart. Remove from the heat. Divide the rice between four serving plates. Top with the green bean and onion stir-fry and the tofu. Sprinkle over sesame seeds, drizzle with some oil and tamari sauce, and serve warm.

BEEF AND EDAMAME STIR-FRY

In this quick and easy recipe, tender sirloin steak is stir-fried with a homemade sauce and fresh vegetables. Served over wholegrain freekeh, it makes for a healthy alternative to the traditional beef stir-fry.

SERVES 4 · PREP 10 MINS · COOK 25 MINS

225g (8oz) uncooked freekeh

1 tbsp light olive oil

450g (1lb) beef sirloin steak, cut into strips

225g (8oz) carrots, shredded

225g (8oz) frozen shelled edamame

175ml (6fl oz) low-sodium soy sauce

60ml (2fl oz) beef stock

60ml (2fl oz) rice vinegar

½ tbsp cornflour, mixed with a little warm water

1 tsp freshly grated root ginger

½ tsp freshly ground black pepper

handful of chopped spring onions, to garnish

1 Place the freekeh and 750ml (1¼ pints) of water in a large, lidded saucepan over a medium heat. Bring to the boil, then reduce the heat to a simmer. Cover and cook for 20–25 minutes, until almost all the water has been absorbed. Remove from the heat, drain any excess water, and set aside.

2 Meanwhile, heat the oil in a large, lidded frying pan over a medium heat. Add the beef and cook for about 1 minute, stirring occasionally. Remove with a slotted spoon and set aside. Add the carrots and edamame to the pan, cover, and cook for about 5 minutes, stirring occasionally.

3 Place the soy sauce, beef stock, rice vinegar, cornflour, ginger, and pepper in a bowl. Whisk until well combined. Pour the liquid mixture into the pan. Then add the beef, stir well to combine, and bring to the boil. Cook, stirring frequently, for a further 10–12 minutes, or until the sauce thickens slightly. Remove from the heat. Divide the freekeh between four serving bowls and top with the stir-fry. Serve hot, garnished with spring onions.

EGG-FRIED MILLET

Wholesome and fluffy millet replaces the standard rice in this egg-fried classic.

SERVES 2 · PREP 10 MINS · COOK 30 MINS

100g (3½oz) uncooked millet

2 eggs

1 tsp sesame oil

2 tbsp light olive oil

4 spring onions, chopped into rounds

100g (3½oz) beansprouts

75g (2½oz) frozen peas, defrosted

2 tsp soy sauce

1 Place the millet in a large saucepan, cover with 120ml (4fl oz) of water, and bring to the boil. Then reduce the heat to a simmer and cook for 10 minutes or until the millet is tender and fluffy. Remove from the heat and use a fork to fluff up the millet. Set aside to cool.

2 Place the eggs and sesame oil in a bowl, whisk to combine, and set aside. Heat the olive oil in a frying pan. Add the millet and cook for 3 minutes, stirring constantly. Then add the spring onions, beansprouts, and peas. Cook, stirring frequently, for a further 3 minutes.

3 Move the millet and vegetables to one side of the pan and add the egg mixture. Cook for 1–2 minutes, without stirring, until it is set. Then use a wooden spoon to break up the egg and mix with the millet and vegetables.

4 Cook, stirring frequently, for about 3 minutes or until the egg is fully cooked and well combined. Remove from the heat. Add the soy sauce and mix well. Season to taste, if needed, and serve hot.

CHINESE CHICKEN WITH BROCCOLI OVER KAMUT

This popular Chinese dish gets a makeover with the addition of protein-rich kamut.

SERVES 4 · PREP 10 MINS, PLUS SOAKING · COOK 50 MINS

200g (7oz) uncooked kamut

1 tbsp rapeseed oil

450g (1lb) chicken breasts, cut into 5mm (¼in) thick strips

130g (4¾oz) broccoli, steamed

1 tsp freshly ground black pepper

FOR THE SAUCE

120ml (4fl oz) low-sodium soy sauce

180ml (6fl oz) chicken stock

2 tbsp cornflour

2 tsp ground ginger

1 tbsp sesame oil

1 Place the kamut in a large bowl and cover with water. Leave to soak for 8 hours. Then drain, rinse under running water, and drain again.

2 Place the kamut in a large saucepan, cover with 750ml (1¼ pints) of water, and bring to the boil. Reduce the heat to a medium-low and cook for 45 minutes or until tender. Then remove from the heat and drain any remaining water. Set aside.

3 For the sauce, place all the ingredients in a bowl and whisk to combine. Heat the oil in a large frying pan over a medium heat. Add the chicken and cook for about 5 minutes, turning over once or twice, until no longer pink on the outside.

4 Add the broccoli and sauce to the pan and season with the pepper. Cover and cook for about 7 minutes or until the sauce has thickened. Remove from the heat. Serve the kamut hot, topped with the chicken and broccoli.

VEGETABLE-FRIED FARRO

in this wholegrain twist on the classic stir-fry recipe, farro replaces the usual starchy white rice. its flavour is deepened by the fact that is toasted first, before being cooked as normal.

SERVES 3 · PREP 15 MINS · COOK 30 MINS

1 tbsp extra virgin olive oil

150g (5½oz) cracked farro

1 garlic clove, sliced

salt

FOR THE VEGETABLES

2 tbsp grapeseed oil

1 garlic clove, crushed

1 tsp grated fresh root ginger

3 spring onions, thinly sliced

1 carrot, finely diced

1 red pepper, deseeded and finely diced

100g (3½oz) sugar snap peas

2 tbsp tamari or low-sodium soy sauce

1 large egg, lightly beaten

1 Heat the olive oil in a saucepan over a medium heat. Add the farro and garlic, season with salt, and cook for 5 minutes, stirring frequently. Then add 1 litre (1¾ pints) of water and bring to the boil. Reduce the heat to a simmer, cover, and cook for 20 minutes. Remove from the heat, drain any remaining water, and set aside.

2 For the vegetables, heat 1 tablespoon of the grapeseed oil in a large frying pan over a medium heat. Add the garlic, ginger, and onions and cook for 2 minutes, stirring frequently. Then add the carrots, peppers, peas, and 1 tablespoon of the tamari. Mix well and cook for 3–4 minutes or until the vegetables are just softened.

3 Move the vegetables to the side and pour in the egg. Cook the egg for 2 minutes, stirring frequently. Then stir to mix the egg with the vegetables. Add the farro and the remaining oil and tamari. Cook for a further 2 minutes, stirring frequently. Remove from the heat and serve hot.

sugar snap peas

TURKEY AND BALSAMiC STiR-FRY WiTH FARRO

Full of Mediterranean flavours, this dish is light yet satisfying. The stir-fried vegetables add a refreshing crunch, complementing the nuttiness of the farro and the tender and subtle taste of the marinated turkey.

SERVES 3 · PREP 10 MiNS, PLUS SOAKING AND MARiNATING · COOK 55 MiNS

100g (3½oz) uncooked farro

2 turkey steaks, about 125g (4½oz) each, sliced into 2cm (¾in) wide strips

1 red or orange pepper, deseeded and cut into strips

1 red onion, roughly chopped

1 courgette, sliced into rounds

1 tbsp light olive oil

handful of basil leaves, to serve

FOR THE MARINADE

3 tbsp balsamic vinegar

1½ tbsp light olive oil

1 garlic clove, finely chopped

1 tsp mixed Italian seasoning

pinch of salt

1 Place the farro in a large bowl and cover with water. Leave to soak for 8 hours or up to 24 hours. Then drain any remaining water and rinse under running water. Drain well and set aside.

2 For the marinade, place all the ingredients in a small bowl and mix to combine. Place the turkey in a plastic bag. Place the red peppers, onions, and courgettes in a separate plastic bag. Divide the marinade equally between the two bags. Then seal the bags and shake lightly to coat. Place in the fridge to marinate for at least 2 hours.

3 Meanwhile, place the farro in a saucepan and cover with water. Bring to the boil, then reduce the heat to a simmer, and cover. Cook for 30–40 minutes or until tender. Remove from the heat and set aside.

4 Heat the oil in a large saucepan over a medium-high heat. Add the turkey, reserving the marinade. Cook, stirring frequently, for about 3 minutes or until cooked through. Then add the vegetables, reserving the marinade. Cook, stirring frequently, for 5 minutes, making sure they stay crunchy and do not overcook.

5 Increase the heat to high. Add all of the reserved marinade to the pan and cook for 3 minutes, stirring frequently, until reduced to a sticky glaze. Add a splash of water if it starts to stick to the bottom. Reduce the heat, add the farro, and stir well to combine. Remove from the heat, garnish with basil, and serve hot.

BEEF, BROCCOLI, AND COCONUT STIR-FRY WITH BULGUR WHEAT

A flavoursome dish that combines beef with creamy bulgur wheat and crunchy broccoli.

SERVES 2 · PREP 10 MINS · COOK 20 MINS

125g (4½oz) uncooked bulgur wheat

1 tbsp vegetable or coconut oil

2.5cm (1in) piece of fresh root ginger, finely chopped

300g (10oz) beef steak, cut into strips

200g (7oz) broccoli, cut into small florets

90ml (3fl oz) full-fat coconut milk

2 tbsp soy sauce, plus extra if needed

salt and freshly ground black pepper

1 Place the bulgur wheat in a large, lidded saucepan. Add 600ml (1 pint) of water and bring to the boil. Then reduce the heat to a simmer, cover, and cook for 15 minutes or until all the water has been absorbed and the bulgur wheat is tender.

2 Heat the oil in a large frying pan over a medium heat. Add the ginger and sauté for 3 minutes. Add the beef and cook for 5 minutes, stirring occasionally. Then add the broccoli, mix well, and cook for 3–5 minutes, stirring frequently. Add the bulgur wheat, coconut milk, and soy sauce and mix well.

3 Cook for 2–3 minutes, stirring frequently, until the beef is cooked through and some of the milk has been absorbed. Make sure the broccoli is still crunchy. Season to taste, if needed, and add more soy sauce if required. Remove from the heat. Drizzle with soy sauce and serve immediately.

PINEAPPLE AND PORK STIR-FRY

This recipes brings together pork, pineapple, and millet in a great combination of Asian flavours.

SERVES 4 · PREP 10 MINS · COOK 30 MINS

200g (7oz) uncooked millet

115g (4oz) carrots, sliced into batons

115g (4oz) mangetout

60ml (2fl oz) low-sodium vegetable stock, plus extra if needed

2 tbsp low-sodium soy sauce

2 tbsp seasoned rice vinegar

1 tbsp cornflour

2 tsp light olive oil

2.5cm (1in) piece of fresh root ginger, grated

2 garlic cloves, crushed

5 spring onions, chopped

450g (1lb) boneless pork chops, cut into thin strips

115g (4oz) pineapple, chopped

1 Place 500ml (16fl oz) of water in a large, lidded saucepan and bring to the boil. Then stir in the millet, cover, and reduce the heat to medium-low. Cook for 15 minutes, until almost all the water has been absorbed. Remove from the heat.

2 Meanwhile, place the carrots and mangetout in a steamer and steam for 10 minutes or until softened. Remove and set aside. For the sauce, place the stock, soy sauce, rice vinegar, and cornflour in a bowl. Whisk until well combined and set aside.

3 Heat the oil in a large frying pan over a medium-high heat. Add the ginger, garlic, and spring onions and cook for 1 minute, stirring occasionally. Then add the pork and cook for 5–6 minutes, stirring occasionally, until well browned. Pour the sauce over and stir to coat. Stir in the mangetout and carrots.

4 Cook for 2–3 minutes, adding more stock if needed, until the sauce thickens and coats the back of a spoon. Stir in the pineapple and remove from the heat. Serve hot over the millet.

TOFU AND KAMUT STIR-FRY

Meaty tofu makes a great vegan alternative in this nutty stir-fry, while the vegetables add lots of crunchy texture and the marinade offers a sweet and sour piquancy.

SERVES 2 · PREP 15 MINS, PLUS MARINATING AND SOAKING · COOK 1 HR

400g (14oz) plain firm tofu, drained

100g (3½oz) uncooked kamut

3 tbsp vegetable oil

1 carrot, cut into matchsticks

1 red pepper, deseeded and cut into thin slices

50g (1¾oz) beansprouts

4 spring onions, thinly sliced

salt and freshly ground black pepper

FOR THE MARINADE

4 tbsp soy sauce, plus extra if needed

2 tbsp honey

5cm (2in) piece of fresh root ginger, finely chopped

2 garlic cloves, finely chopped

1 For the marinade, place all the ingredients in a bowl and mix to combine. Cut the tofu into 2cm (¾in) cubes and place in a plastic bag. Pour half the marinade over, seal the bag, and shake lightly to coat. Leave to marinate in the fridge for 3–4 hours. Reserve the remaining marinade

2 Place the kamut in a large bowl, cover with water, and leave to soak for 8 hours. Then drain and rinse under running water. Drain and place in a large, lidded saucepan. Cover with water and bring to the boil. Then reduce the heat to a simmer, cover, and cook for 45 minutes or until tender. Remove from the heat and drain.

3 Heat 2 tablespoons of the oil in a frying pan over a medium-high heat. Add the tofu and sauté for about 10 minutes, until evenly browned. Remove with a slotted spoon. Pour the remaining oil into the pan. Add the carrots and red peppers and cook for about 2 minutes, stirring frequently.

4 Add the beansprouts and cook for about 3 minutes, stirring frequently. Add the kamut, tofu, and reserved marinade and combine well. Then add the onions and cook for 2 minutes, stirring frequently. Season to taste, adding more soy sauce if needed, and remove from the heat. Serve hot.

GRAIN EXCHANGE

You could replace the kamut with any of the following grains. Use the same amount of grain.

wheat berries

spelt

barley

why not try ...

You could try adding the same amount of **chicken** instead of the tofu or use the same quantity of **yellow peppers** in place of the red peppers.

PRAWN AND ASPARAGUS STiR-FRY WiTH POLENTA

In this satisfying dish, prawns and asparagus are stir-fried in a light white wine sauce and served over creamy, cheesy polenta. Quick and easy, it is perfect for dinner or even impressing your friends!

SERVES 4 · PREP 10 MiNS · COOK 20 MiNS

2 tbsp extra virgin olive oil

3 garlic cloves, crushed

6–8 spring onions, white and green parts, finely chopped

450g (1lb) asparagus, ends removed and cut into 2.5cm (1in) pieces

450g (1lb) prawns, peeled and deveined

60ml (2fl oz) white wine

salt and freshly ground black pepper

150g (5½oz) uncooked polenta

100g (3½oz) freshly grated Asiago or Parmesan cheese, plus extra to garnish

1 lemon, sliced, to serve

1 Heat the oil in a large frying pan over a medium heat. Add the garlic, spring onions, and asparagus. Cook for 5 minutes, stirring occasionally, until the onions have softened. Then add the prawns and cook for 3 minutes, stirring, until just beginning to turn pink.

2 Pour in the wine and stir to combine. Cook for a further 2–3 minutes or until the prawns are cooked through and pink. Remove from the heat and season to taste, if needed.

3 Meanwhile, place 750ml (1¼ pints) water and ¼ teaspoon salt in a large saucepan and bring to the boil. Stir in the polenta and reduce the heat to medium-low. Cook for about 5 minutes, stirring occasionally. Remove from the heat and stir in the cheese.

4 Divide the polenta evenly between four plates and top with one-quarter of the prawn and asparagus stir-fry. Garnish with cheese and serve hot with lemon slices.

NOURISHING RISOTTOS AND PILAFS

ITALIAN TOMATO BARLEY RISOTTO

Bursting with italian flavours, this healthy risotto gets its interesting texture from slow-cooked pearl barley. The green olives and basil leaves also make great additions to the traditional tomato sauce.

SERVES 4 · PREP 10 MINS · COOK 45 MINS

1 tbsp light olive oil

1 onion, finely chopped

2 garlic cloves, crushed

300g (10oz) pearl barley, rinsed

375ml (13fl oz) tomato passata

600ml (1 pint) vegetable stock

1 tsp Italian seasoning

400g can cannellini beans, drained

120g (4¼oz) green olives, pitted and halved

salt and freshly ground black pepper

handful of basil leaves, to garnish

1 Heat the oil in a large, lidded saucepan over a medium-high heat. Add the onions and garlic and cook for about 5 minutes or until the onions are softened. Then add the barley to the pan, stir to coat with the oil, and cook for a further 2 minutes.

2 Add the passata, stock, and Italian seasoning to the pan. Stir well and reduce the heat to a simmer. Cover and cook for 30 minutes or until most of the liquid has been absorbed and the barley is chewy. Make sure you stir the risotto occasionally to prevent the barley from sticking to the bottom of the pan.

3 Stir the beans into the risotto and cook for a further 5 minutes. Remove from the heat and stir in the olives, making sure they are evenly distributed. Season to taste, garnish with basil leaves, and serve hot.

GRAIN EXCHANGE
You can use the same amount of any one of the following grains in place of the barley.

wheat berries

spelt

farro

why not try...
Try the same amount of **haricot beans, chickpeas,** or **borlotti beans** instead of the cannellini beans.

TEFF AND BUTTERNUT SQUASH RISOTTO

The sweetness of roasted butternut squash combines with aromatic sage and rich double cream in this classic risotto that uses teff in place of the more usual rice. It's a deliciously warming dish for a cool autumn day.

SERVES 2 · PREP 20 MINS · COOK 1 HR 10 MINS

1 butternut squash, about 500g (1lb 2oz), deseeded and diced into 1–2cm (½–¾in) pieces

2 tbsp light olive oil

1 tbsp unsalted butter

1 small onion, finely chopped

1 garlic clove, finely chopped

100g (3½oz) uncooked teff

500ml (16fl oz) chicken stock

2 tbsp double cream

15g (½oz) freshly grated Parmesan cheese, plus extra to serve

¼ tsp dried sage

salt and freshly ground black pepper

2 tbsp chopped basil, to garnish

1 Preheat the oven to 200°C (400°F/Gas 6). Place the butternut squash in a large baking tray, drizzle over 1 tablespoon of the oil, and toss to coat. Place the tray in the oven and bake for about 40 minutes or until the squash is tender but still has some bite to it.

2 Heat the butter and remaining oil in a large frying pan over a medium heat. Add the onions and garlic and sauté for about 5 minutes or until the onions are soft and translucent. Then add the teff and stir to coat in the butter and oil.

3 Add 250ml (9fl oz) of the stock, a ladleful at a time, stirring constantly, allowing the liquid to be fully absorbed before adding more. Then add half of the butternut squash and stir to mix.

4 Pour in the remaining stock, a little at a time, stirring constantly. Cook for 15–20 minutes, until all the stock has been absorbed and the squash has started to break down. Then add the cream and Parmesan and stir to mix.

5 Add the sage and remaining butternut squash to the pan and stir to mix. Remove from the heat and season to taste. Garnish the risotto with basil and Parmesan and serve hot.

GARLICKY SPINACH AND SPELT RISOTTO

Easy to make and quick to prepare, this hearty risotto contains the goodness of spinach, garlic, and wholegrain spelt and is a great nutrient boost for when you're feeling a little under the weather.

SERVES 2 · PREP 10 MINS · COOK 30 MINS

1 tbsp light olive oil

1 tbsp unsalted butter

1 small onion, finely chopped

4 garlic cloves, finely chopped

100g (3½oz) pearled spelt

500ml (16fl oz) hot chicken stock

85g (3oz) spinach, rough stems removed and roughly chopped

2 tbsp double cream

15g (½oz) freshly grated Parmesan cheese, plus extra to serve

1 Heat the oil and butter in a large frying pan over a medium heat. Add the onions and garlic and sauté for about 5 minutes or until the onions are translucent. Then add the spelt, stir to coat in the oil and butter, and sauté for a further 3 minutes.

2 Add the stock a ladleful at a time, stirring constantly, allowing the liquid to be fully absorbed before adding more. Cook for 10 minutes, stirring frequently, until three-quarters of the liquid has been absorbed. Then add the spinach a handful at a time, letting it wilt and reduce with the stock before adding more.

3 Cook, stirring frequently, for a further 10 minutes, until all the stock has been absorbed and the spinach has wilted. Then add the cream and Parmesan, stir well to combine, and season to taste. Remove from the heat. Sprinkle over some Parmesan and serve hot.

GRAIN EXCHANGE

For a change, try replacing the spelt with the same amount of either of the following grains.

barley

wheat berries

APPLE, WALNUT, GOJI BERRY, CHICKEN, AND WHEAT BERRY PILAF

This filling pilaf uniquely combines crisp apple and chewy wheat berries with nuts and sweet berries. Add some tender chicken to the mix and you're left with a healthy and filling meal.

SERVES 4 · PREP 15 MINS, PLUS SOAKING · COOK 50 MINS

200g (7oz) uncooked
　wheat berries

60g (2oz) goji berries

20g (¾oz) walnuts, chopped

1 tbsp light olive oil

2 chicken breasts, diced

1 onion, finely sliced

1 garlic clove, crushed

1 large dessert apple, grated

salt

handful of flat-leaf parsley,
　finely chopped

handful of basil leaves,
　finely chopped

1 Place the wheat berries in a large saucepan, cover with water, and bring to the boil. Then reduce the heat to a simmer and cook for 30–40 minutes or until they are tender.

2 Meanwhile, place the goji berries in a small bowl, cover with water, and leave to soak for 10 minutes. Heat a large frying pan over a medium heat. Add the walnuts and lightly toast for 3–4 minutes. Remove from the heat and set aside.

3 Increase the heat to medium-high and pour the oil into the pan. Add the chicken and cook for 10 minutes, stirring frequently. Then add the onions and garlic to the pan. Cook for a further 5 minutes, stirring occasionally, until the chicken is cooked through and the onions have softened. Remove from the heat.

4 Drain the wheat berries, add them to the pan, and mix to combine with the chicken and onions. Drain the goji berries and discard the water. Add the goji berries, walnuts, and apples to the pilaf and mix lightly to combine. Taste and adjust the seasoning, if needed. Garnish with the herbs and serve hot.

GRAIN EXCHANGE

For a change, try using the same amount of any one of the following grains in place of the wheat berries.

barley

spelt

farro

why not try...

Instead of the goji berries, try some **dried cranberries**, or swap **pecans** for the walnuts. You could even try adding turkey instead of the chicken.

SWEET POTATO, CRANBERRY, AND PECAN FARRO

An autumn-inspired recipe, this pilaf-like dish is packed with the rich flavour of sweet potato, which is well paired with the nutty and creamy farro, crunchy pecans, and the tangy apple cider dressing.

SERVES 4 · PREP 15 MINS, PLUS OVERNIGHT SOAKING · COOK 1 HR 10 MINS

200g (7oz) uncooked farro

2 sweet potatoes, cut into 1cm (½in) cubes

2 tbsp light olive oil

1 onion, finely chopped

1 tsp ground cinnamon

½ tsp ground cumin

100g (3½oz) dried cranberries

100g (3½oz) pecans, roughly chopped

4 tbsp roughly chopped flat-leaf parsley

FOR THE DRESSING

3 tbsp extra virgin olive oil

1 tbsp apple cider vinegar

1 Place the farro in a bowl and cover with water. Leave to soak overnight or for up to 8 hours. Then drain, rinse under running water, and drain well again.

2 Place the farro in a large, lidded saucepan, cover with water, and bring to the boil. Then reduce the heat to a simmer, cover, and cook for 30 minutes, until tender. Remove from the heat and drain any remaining water. Set aside.

3 Meanwhile, preheat the oven to 200°C (400°F/Gas 6). Place the potatoes in a baking tray and toss with 1 tablespoon of the oil. Bake for 30–40 minutes, until tender.

4 Heat the remaining oil in a large frying pan over a medium heat. Add the onions and cook for about 5 minutes, stirring frequently, until softened. Then add the cinnamon and cumin and cook for a further 2 minutes, stirring frequently.

5 Add the farro and sweet potatoes and stir to combine. Then add the cranberries, stir to mix, and cook for a further 2 minutes, stirring frequently. Remove from the heat.

6 For the dressing, combine the ingredients in a small bowl and pour over the pilaf. Toss to mix, sprinkle over the pecans and parsley, and serve hot.

GRAIN EXCHANGE

Try replacing the farro with the same amount of either of the following grains.

spelt

barley

GOAT'S CHEESE, BALSAMIC VINEGAR, AND BUCKWHEAT RISOTTO WITH PARMA HAM

Buckwheat makes a delicious and healthy substitute for rice in this risotto. The pairing of creamy melted goat's cheese with tangy balsamic vinegar proves to be a real treat for the taste buds.

SERVES 2 · PREP 15 MINS · COOK 30 MINS

3 tbsp olive oil

2 garlic cloves, crushed

1 onion, diced

175g (6oz) uncooked buckwheat

750ml (1¼ pints) chicken stock

40g (1½oz) butter

salt and freshly ground black pepper

60g (2oz) goat's cheese

1 tbsp balsamic vinegar

5 slices Parma ham, chopped

1 tbsp roughly chopped flat-leaf parsley

1 Heat the oil in a large saucepan over a medium heat. Add the garlic and the onions and cook for 3–4 minutes, stirring frequently, until softened. Then add the buckwheat and cook for a further 2 minutes, stirring frequently.

2 Pour in the stock, stir to mix, and bring to the boil. Then reduce the heat to a simmer and cook for about 15 minutes, stirring frequently. Then add the butter and mix well to combine. Cook for a further 5 minutes, until almost all of the stock has been absorbed. Add more stock or water to the risotto if it starts to become dry too quickly.

3 Remove from the heat and season to taste. Add the goat's cheese and vinegar and mix until the cheese has melted and is well incorporated. Sprinkle over the Parma ham and parsley and stir to mix. Serve hot.

CHERRY AND PiSTACHiO FREEKEH PiLAF

This tasty freekeh dish is made with warming, aromatic spices and mixed with dried cherries and pistachios, creating a savoury and sweet pilaf unlike any you've had before.

SERVES 4 · PREP 5 MiNS · COOK 20–25 MiNS

200g (7oz) uncooked freekeh

8 cardamom pods

8 whole cloves

1 tbsp oil

1 onion, finely chopped

1 tsp ground cinnamon

pinch of salt

100g (3½oz) dried cherries, roughly chopped

100g (3½oz) pistachios, roughly chopped

FOR THE DRESSING

3 tbsp olive oil

2 tbsp lemon juice

pinch of salt

1 Place the freekeh in a large saucepan, cover with 1 litre (1¾ pints) of water, and place over a medium heat. Add the cardamom and cloves and simmer for 20 minutes or until all the water has been absorbed. Drain any remaining water and remove and discard the cardamom and cloves. Set aside.

2 Meanwhile, heat the oil in a large frying pan over a medium heat. Add the onions and cook for 5–10 minutes, stirring occasionally, until softened and translucent. Then add the cinnamon and cook for a further 2 minutes.

3 For the dressing, place all the ingredients in a small bowl and mix to combine. Add the freekeh to the onion mixture, season with the salt, and stir to mix. Then add the cherries and pistachios and stir until evenly distributed. Remove from the heat. Serve hot with the dressing drizzled over.

GRAiN EXCHANGE

For a variation, in place of the freekeh, use 120g (4¼oz) of **bulgur wheat** and cook it in 600ml (1 pint) of water.

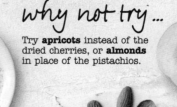

why not try...

Try **apricots** instead of the dried cherries, or **almonds** in place of the pistachios.

NUTTY SPICED BULGUR WHEAT PILAF
WITH RAISINS

Delicately flavoured with spices, this light and aromatic pilaf makes the perfect supper dish. The toasted almonds and raisins add texture and really complement the creamy taste of the bulgur wheat.

SERVES 4 · PREP 10 MINS · COOK 45 MINS

125g (4½oz) uncooked bulgur wheat

60g (2oz) flaked almonds

1 tbsp light olive oil

1 onion, finely chopped

1 tsp ground cinnamon

2 tbsp ground cumin

85g (3oz) raisins

200ml (7fl oz) vegetable stock

salt and freshly ground black pepper

4 tbsp chopped flat-leaf parsley, to garnish

1 Place the bulgur wheat in a large saucepan and cover with 600ml (1 pint) of water. Bring to the boil, then reduce the heat to a simmer. Cook for 20–30 minutes or until all the water has been absorbed and the bulgur wheat is soft. Remove from the heat, drain any remaining water, and set aside.

2 Heat a non-stick frying pan over a medium-high heat. Add the almonds and toast them for about 5 minutes, stirring frequently, until golden brown. Remove from the heat and set aside.

3 Heat the oil in a saucepan over a medium heat. Add the onions and cook for about 5 minutes, stirring frequently, until softened. Then add the cinnamon and cumin and cook, stirring frequently, for a further 2 minutes.

4 Add the raisins and bulgur wheat and mix well to combine. Cook for a further 2 minutes, adding the stock if the mixture gets too dry or sticks to the bottom of the pan. Remove from the heat and season to taste. Sprinkle over the almonds and garnish with parsley. Serve hot.

almonds

MUSHROOM BARLEY RISOTTO

Pearl barley makes a good substitute for rice in this earthy mushroom risotto. Be sure to cook it slowly to get the right texture.

SERVES 4 · PREP 10 MINS · COOK 45 MINS

1 tbsp light olive oil

1 small onion, diced

15 chestnut mushrooms, thinly sliced

225g (8oz) uncooked pearl barley

120ml (4fl oz) white wine

1 litre (1¾ pints) hot chicken stock

115g (4oz) freshly grated Parmesan cheese

1 tbsp finely chopped sage

sea salt and freshly ground black pepper

1 Heat the oil in a large non-stick frying pan over a low heat. Add the onions and mushrooms. Cook, stirring frequently, for about 10 minutes or until the onions are softened and the mushrooms have browned and released their juices.

2 Increase the heat to medium, stir in the barley, and cook for 1 minute. Pour in the wine and cook for 5 minutes or until fully absorbed. Gradually add the stock, a ladleful at a time, stirring constantly, allowing the liquid to be fully absorbed before adding more.

3 Cook for 25–30 minutes, stirring frequently. Then stir in the Parmesan and sage and season to taste. Mix well to combine and remove from the heat. Serve immediately.

PEA AND GOAT'S CHEESE AMARANTH RISOTTO

A richly flavoured risotto made with spring peas, salty goat's cheese, and earthy amaranth.

SERVES 2 · PREP 5 MINS · COOK 40 MINS

1 tbsp walnut oil

1 onion, finely chopped

1 garlic clove, finely chopped

250g (9oz) uncooked amaranth

50g (1¾oz) uncooked teff

750ml (1¼ pints) hot vegetable stock

200g (7oz) frozen peas

50g (1¾oz) soft goat's cheese

salt and freshly ground black pepper

1 Heat the oil in a large non-stick saucepan over a medium heat. Add the onions and garlic and cook, stirring frequently, for about 5 minutes or until the onions are softened.

2 Add the amaranth, teff, and stock and stir to combine. Bring to a simmer, then reduce the heat to a medium. Cook, stirring frequently, for about 25 minutes.

3 Add the peas and cook for a further 10 minutes or until all the stock has been absorbed and the amaranth and teff are soft and creamy. Sprinkle over the cheese and season to taste. Stir well to combine and remove from the heat. Serve hot.

SPICY PRAWNS WITH LIME, FARRO, AND CORIANDER

This refreshing dish makes an ideal supper, marrying luscious prawns with creamy avocado, sweet baby plum tomatoes, and nutty farro. The chilli flakes and lime juice add just the right amount of piquancy.

SERVES 4 · PREP 10 MINS · COOK 1 HR 10 MINS

175g (6oz) uncooked farro

salt and freshly ground black pepper

2 tbsp olive oil

3 garlic cloves, crushed

450g (1lb) prawns, peeled and deveined

2 tomatoes, diced

½ tsp chilli flakes

1 avocado, pitted and diced

150g (5½ oz) baby plum tomatoes, halved

2 tbsp finely chopped coriander leaves

60ml (2fl oz) lime juice

2 lemons or limes, halved, to serve (optional)

1 Place the farro in a large, lidded saucepan. Pour over 560ml (19fl oz) of water and add ½ teaspoon salt. Bring to the boil over a medium heat. Then reduce the heat to medium-low, cover, and cook for 50–60 minutes, until tender. Remove from the heat, drain any remaining water, and transfer to a large bowl. Set aside.

2 Meanwhile, heat the oil in a large, lidded frying pan over a medium heat. Add the garlic and cook for about 1 minute, stirring, until fragrant. Then add the prawns, tomatoes, and chilli flakes and stir well. Cover and cook for about 10 minutes or until the prawns are pink and cooked through. Season to taste and remove from the heat.

3 Add the avocado, baby plum tomatoes, and coriander to the farro. Mix well to combine. Drizzle over the lime juice and toss lightly to coat. Taste and adjust the seasoning and divide evenly between four plates. Top with the spicy prawns and serve hot with the lemons or limes, if using.

CURRIED SORGHUM PILAF
WITH COCONUT

Cauliflower has been eaten for hundreds of years and became popular during the 16th and 17th centuries, when it was considered a delicacy. Combined with the curry spices and creamy coconut milk, it makes for a great flavour match.

SERVES 2 · PREP 10 MINS · COOK 1 HR 15 MINS

100g (3½oz) uncooked sorghum

150g (5½oz) cauliflower, chopped into florets

20g (¾oz) coconut flakes

1 tbsp light olive oil

1 onion, finely chopped

2 tsp mild curry powder

85ml (2¾fl oz) full-fat coconut milk

salt and freshly ground black pepper

2 tbsp chopped coriander leaves, to garnish

1 Place the sorghum in a large saucepan, cover with water, and bring to the boil. Then reduce the heat to a simmer and cook for 45 minutes–1 hour or until the sorghum is tender, but still chewy. Remove from the heat and set aside.

2 Place the cauliflower in a steamer and steam for 10 minutes or until tender when pierced with a fork. Set aside. Heat a frying pan over a medium-high heat. Add the coconut flakes and toast for about 5 minutes, stirring frequently, until lightly toasted. Remove from the heat and set aside.

3 Pour the oil into the pan and reduce the heat to medium. Add the onion and sauté for about 5 minutes or until softened. Then add the curry powder and sauté for about 2 minutes. Add the cauliflower and sorghum and mix well to combine.

4 Add the coconut milk to the pan. Mix well and cook for a further 2 minutes. Then add half the coconut flakes and mix well to combine. Season to taste and remove from the heat. Sprinkle over the remaining coconut, garnish with coriander, and serve hot.

GRAIN EXCHANGE

For a change, try replacing the sorghum with the same amount of either of these grains.

kamut

millet

BACON, KALE, AND BARLEY RISOTTO

The perfect comfort food and packed full of goodness, this risotto is amazingly tasty. The creamy barley makes a great base for the contrast of the salty bacon and the nutrient-rich kale.

SERVES 2 · PREP 15 MINS, PLUS OVERNIGHT SOAKING · COOK 40 MINS

150g (5½oz) uncooked pearl barley

1 tbsp butter, room temperature

1½ tbsp light olive oil

1 small onion, finely chopped

1 garlic clove, finely chopped

500ml (16fl oz) hot vegetable stock

30g (1oz) kale, stems removed and roughly chopped

2 tbsp double cream

15g (½oz) freshly grated Parmesan cheese, plus extra to serve

4 rashers of thick-cut unsmoked back bacon, cut into strips

salt and freshly ground black pepper

1 Place the barley in a bowl, cover with water and leave to soak overnight or for up to 8 hours. Then drain well and rinse under running water. Drain again and set aside.

2 Heat the butter and 1 tablespoon of the oil in a frying pan over a medium heat. Add the onions and garlic and sauté for about 5 minutes or until the onions are translucent.

3 Add the barley, stir to coat in the oil and butter, and cook for 3 minutes, stirring frequently. Then add the stock a ladleful at a time, stirring constantly, allowing the liquid to be fully absorbed before adding more.

4 When more than half the stock has been absorbed, add the kale, a handful at a time, and stir well to combine. Cook for 20–25 minutes or until the kale has wilted and all the stock has been absorbed. Then stir in the cream and Parmesan.

5 Meanwhile, heat the remaining oil in a small frying pan over a medium-high heat. Add the bacon and fry for 7 minutes, until cooked through and starting to crisp up. Remove with a slotted spoon, add to the risotto, and mix well to combine. Season with salt and pepper, sprinkle with Parmesan, and serve hot.

ROASTED VEGETABLE FARRO RISOTTO

This rich and delicious risotto uses farro for its chewy texture and slightly sweet flavour. The addition of roasted vegetables makes this a warm and satisfying meal.

SERVES 4 · PREP 15 MINS · COOK 40 MINS

3 tbsp light olive oil

1 small onion, finely chopped

150g (5½oz) uncooked farro

120ml (4fl oz) white wine

1 litre (1¾ pints) hot chicken stock

50g (1¾oz) freshly grated Parmesan cheese

1 tbsp finely chopped thyme

sea salt and freshly ground black pepper

1 red pepper, deseeded and thinly sliced

1 courgette, diced

150g (5½oz) cherry tomatoes

1 Preheat the oven to 200°C (400°F/Gas 6). Heat 1 tablespoon of the oil in a large saucepan over a medium heat. Add the onion and cook for about 5 minutes, stirring frequently, until softened. Then add the farro, stir to mix, and cook gently for 1–2 minutes.

2 Stir the wine into the pan and leave to cook until all the liquid has been absorbed. Then add the stock a ladleful at a time, stirring constantly, allowing the liquid to be fully absorbed before adding more. Once all the liquid has been absorbed, add the Parmesan and thyme, and season to taste. Remove from the heat.

3 Meanwhile, arrange the red peppers, courgette, and tomatoes in a baking tray. Drizzle over the remaining oil and season with salt and pepper. Transfer the tray to the oven and roast the vegetables for 20–25 minutes, stirring occasionally, until cooked through and golden. Stir the roasted vegetables into the risotto and serve immediately.

KAMUT AND FENNEL RISOTTO

Fennel is a member of the celery family and very popular in Mediterranean countries. Kamut has a far nuttier and richer flavour than traditional risotto rice and is the perfect foil for the slight aniseed taste of the fresh fennel.

SERVES 2 · PREP 10 MINS, PLUS OVERNIGHT SOAKING · COOK 1 HR

175g (6oz) uncooked kamut, soaked overnight

750ml (1¼ pints) chicken or vegetable stock

1 tbsp butter

1 tbsp olive oil

1 fennel bulb, diced and fronds reserved

1 onion, diced

1 garlic clove, crushed

120ml (4fl oz) white wine

1 tsp grated lemon zest

30g (1oz) freshly grated Parmesan cheese, plus extra to serve

salt and freshly ground black pepper

1 Place the kamut and stock in a large, lidded saucepan and bring to the boil. Then reduce the heat to a simmer, cover, and cook for about 45 minutes. Remove from the heat. Strain the kamut, reserving any remaining liquid, and set aside.

2 Heat the butter and oil in a large, deep-sided saucepan over a medium heat. Add the fennel and onions and cook for about 5 minutes, stirring frequently, until softened. Then add the garlic and cook for a further 2 minutes.

3 Add the kamut and wine and cook, stirring frequently, until the wine has been absorbed. Then add about 60ml (2fl oz) of the reserved stock and cook, stirring frequently, until the liquid is fully absorbed and the kamut is tender but still has some bite. Check the texture of the kamut frequently and add more stock if needed.

4 Add the lemon zest and Parmesan, stir well to combine, and remove from the heat. Season to taste, garnish with fennel fronds, and sprinkle over some Parmesan. Serve immediately.

fennel bulb

CURRIED LENTIL QUINOA PILAF

With all the flavours of an indian curry that are lifted by the fresh ginger, this filling pilaf is packed full of goodness as the quinoa and lentils make a powerful and nutritious combination.

SERVES 4 · PREP 10 MINS · COOK 40 MINS

2 tbsp olive oil

½ onion, finely chopped

2 garlic cloves, crushed

2 tsp grated fresh root ginger

1 tbsp garam masala

90g (3¼oz) dried lentils, rinsed

90g (3¼oz) quinoa

60g (2oz) frozen peas

salt and freshly ground black pepper

1 Heat the oil in a large, lidded saucepan over a medium heat. Add the onions and cook for 6–8 minutes, stirring frequently, until translucent. Then add the garlic, ginger, and garam masala, stir to combine, and cook for 1 more minute. Add the lentils and 500ml (16fl oz) of water, stir to mix, and bring to the boil.

2 Reduce the heat to medium-low, cover, and cook for about 10 minutes. Then add the quinoa and peas, stir to combine, and cook for a further 20 minutes or until the liquid has been absorbed, the lentils are cooked, and the quinoa is tender. Season to taste and remove from the heat. Serve immediately.

garlic cloves

RED PEPPERS STUFFED WITH ARTICHOKE BARLEY RISOTTO

These lightly roasted sweet red peppers are the perfect vessels for a creamy barley risotto dotted with artichoke hearts and are a delightful change from the conventional stuffed peppers.

SERVES 6 · PREP 10 MINS · COOK 35 MINS

4 tbsp extra virgin olive oil

1 small onion, diced

225g (8oz) uncooked barley

125ml (4¼fl oz) white wine

1 litre (1¾ pints) warm vegetable stock

100g (3½oz) freshly grated Parmesan cheese

350g (12oz) artichoke hearts, chopped

salt and freshly ground black pepper

6 red peppers

1 Heat 2 tablespoons of the oil in a large saucepan over a medium heat. Add the onion and cook, stirring frequently, for 5–10 minutes or until translucent and lightly browned. Then add the barley, stir to mix, and cook for a further 1–2 minutes.

2 Stir the wine into the pan and leave to cook until all the liquid has been absorbed. Then add the stock a ladleful at a time, stirring constantly, allowing the liquid to be fully absorbed before adding more. Once all the stock has been added, cook, stirring constantly, for a further 2–3 minutes or until all the liquid has been absorbed. Remove from the heat, stir in the Parmesan and artichoke hearts, and season to taste.

3 Preheat the oven to 180°C (350°F/Gas 4). Slice the red peppers in half lengthways. Then, core, deseed, and remove the white ribs from the inside and discard. Rub the peppers with the remaining oil and place on a baking sheet lined with foil. Roast in the oven for 15 minutes, until softened. Remove from the heat. Divide the risotto mixture into 6 equal parts and use to fill the peppers. Serve immediately.

CHICKEN-FRIED FREEKEH

Based on the popular Chinese dish of egg-fried rice, this easy-to-make recipe uses freekeh instead of rice as a healthy alternative, with the sesame oil and soy sauce providing the traditional tangy elements.

SERVES 4 · PREP 10 MINS · COOK 35 MINS

200g (7oz) cracked freekeh

1 tbsp olive oil

2 large garlic cloves, crushed

2 spring onions, thinly sliced

225g (8oz) cooked chicken, diced

1 tsp sesame oil

salt and freshly ground black pepper

2 large eggs, lightly beaten

4 tbsp low-sodium soy sauce

1 Rinse the freekeh under running water and drain well. Place in a large saucepan, cover with 1 litre (1¾ pints) of water, and bring to the boil over a high heat. Then reduce the heat to a simmer and cook for 15 minutes, until almost all of the water has been absorbed. Remove from the heat and set aside.

2 Heat the olive oil in a wok or large, non-stick frying pan over a medium heat. Add the garlic and onions and cook for 3–4 minutes, stirring frequently, until the onions are softened.

3 Add the freekeh and stir to incorporate. Then add the chicken and sesame oil, season with salt and pepper, and mix until well combined. Cook for about 4 minutes, stirring frequently, until the chicken is heated through.

4 Move the freekeh mixture to one side of the pan, making a little space in the other. Pour the eggs in and cook for 2–3 minutes, without stirring, until firm. Then stir well to mix and cook for a further 1–2 minutes, until cooked through.

5 Mix the eggs with the freekeh and chicken mixture, scraping up the pan juices, and cook for a further 1–2 minutes or until well combined. Remove from the heat, drizzle over the soy sauce, and mix well. Serve hot.

WHOLESOME BURGERS AND LIGHT MEALS

QUINOA FALAFEL
WITH MINT YOGURT SAUCE

The addition of quinoa to the traditional falafel gives them an added wholegrain goodness and a unique flavour and texture. it is paired here with a fresh and light yogurt sauce to complement the earthy spices.

SERVES 4 · PREP 15 MINS, PLUS CHILLING · COOK 45 MINS

60g (2oz) uncooked quinoa

1 egg

2 garlic cloves

1 tbsp cumin

¼ tsp salt

2 x 400g can chickpeas, drained

4 tbsp chopped coriander leaves

1 tbsp plain flour, for dusting

1–2 tbsp olive oil, plus extra for greasing

FOR THE SAUCE

150g (5½oz) Greek yogurt

4 tbsp chopped mint leaves

juice of 1 lemon

1 Rinse the quinoa under running water, place in a large saucepan, and cover with 170ml (6fl oz) of water. Place the pan over a medium heat and bring to a simmer. Cook the quinoa for 15 minutes or until almost all the water has been absorbed. Remove from the heat, drain any remaining water, and set aside.

2 Place the quinoa, egg, garlic, cumin, salt, and 350g (12oz) of the chickpeas in a food processor. Pulse until well combined. Add the coriander and the remaining chickpeas and pulse lightly for 1 minute, until the chickpeas have broken down but still retain some of their texture. Transfer the mixture to a large bowl and chill in the fridge for 30 minutes.

3 Preheat the oven to 200°C (400°F/Gas 6). Grease and line a baking sheet with greaseproof paper. Divide the falafel mixture into eight equal portions. On a lightly floured surface, roll each portion into a smooth ball and press down lightly to form patty-like shapes.

4 Brush the falafel with a little oil on both sides and place on the baking sheet. Bake in the oven for 20 minutes or until the falafel are well browned and crispy on the outside. Remove from the heat.

5 For the sauce, place all the ingredients in a bowl and mix well. Serve the falafel and mint yogurt sauce with pitta breads and a green salad, if liked.

TEFF STACKS
WITH MEDITERRANEAN VEGETABLES

The versatile teff is used here to make tasty fried patties and combined with the classic Mediterranean trio of aubergine, tomato, and mozzarella. Perfect when served on a warm day with crusty bread and a glass of chilled white wine.

SERVES 4 · PREP 20 MINS, PLUS COOLING · COOK 30 MINS

750ml (1¼ pints) hot vegetable stock

200g (7oz) uncooked teff

1 aubergine, sliced into 8 x 5mm (¼in) wide rounds

salt and freshly ground black pepper

1 tbsp light olive oil, plus extra to serve

2 large tomatoes, sliced into 8 x 5mm (¼in) wide rounds

200g (7oz) mozzarella cheese, sliced into 8 x 5mm (¼in) wide rounds

handful of basil leaves, to garnish

1 Grease and line two 20 x 25cm (8 x 10in) baking trays with greaseproof paper and set aside. Place the stock in a large saucepan and bring to a simmer over a medium-high heat. Then add the teff and stir well to mix.

2 Reduce the heat to medium and cook for 15–20 minutes, stirring frequently to avoid lumps, until the teff thickens to a porridge-like consistency. Remove from the heat. Divide the teff equally between the prepared trays and use a wooden spoon to spread into a smooth and even layer. Set aside to cool and firm up.

3 Place the aubergine slices in a colander, sprinkle with ¼ teaspoon of salt, and set aside to draw out the water. Remove the teff from the baking trays and place on a clean work surface. Cut out eight large rounds using a cookie cutter or the bottom of a glass.

4 Heat a griddle pan over a high heat. Dry the aubergine slices with kitchen paper and grill on the griddle pan for 2 minutes on each side, until lightly chargrilled and tender. Remove from the heat and set aside.

5 Heat the oil in a large frying pan over a medium-high heat. Fry the teff rounds for 2 minutes on each side, until crisp. Set aside. Then fry the tomato slices for 1–2 minutes on each side and remove from the heat.

6 To assemble the stacks, place one teff round on each of four plates. Top each one with a slice of aubergine, tomato, and mozzarella each. Repeat to get two layers of each ingredient. Season with pepper, sprinkle over the basil and drizzle with oil. Serve immediately.

CAULiFLOWER HAZELNUT POLENTA

it may seem fiddly to skin the hazelnuts, but the skins can be quite bitter and will change the taste of the dish if left on. The sweetness of the roasted nuts contrasts well with the cauliflower and the ripeness of the Manchego.

SERVES 4 · PREP 15 MiNS · COOK 30 MiNS

75g (2½oz) hazelnuts

450g (1lb) cauliflower, cut into florets

1 tbsp olive oil

salt and freshly ground black pepper

juice of half a lemon

FOR THE POLENTA

500ml (16fl oz) milk, plus extra if needed

150g (5½oz) coarse polenta

3 tbsp unsalted butter

30g (1oz) grated Manchego cheese, plus extra to serve

handful of flat-leaf parsley, roughly chopped, to garnish

1 Preheat the oven to 180°C (350°F/Gas 4). Spread the hazelnuts out on a baking sheet, place in the oven, and toast for 10–15 minutes or until they are well browned with the skins peeling off. Leave them to cool slightly. Then place them between two pieces of kitchen paper and rub to remove the skins. Roughly chop the hazelnuts and set aside.

2 Increase the heat to 200°C (400°F/Gas 6). Place the cauliflower on a large baking sheet, drizzle over the oil, and season well. Place in the oven and roast for 30 minutes, stirring occasionally, until golden brown and cooked through. Remove from the heat, drizzle over the lemon juice, and set aside.

3 For the polenta, place the milk and 500ml (16fl oz) of water in a large, lidded saucepan. Add ¼ teaspoon salt and a good grinding of pepper. Bring to the boil, then reduce the heat to medium-low. Gradually add one-third of the polenta, stirring constantly, until well combined. Then add the remaining polenta, stirring constantly, and cook for about 10 minutes or until it is well combined and smooth.

4 Reduce the heat to low and cover partially. Cook for a further 15 minutes, stirring occasionally to ensure it does not stick to the bottom, until it is creamy. Add a little more water or milk to the pan if the polenta seems too thick. Then stir in the butter and cheese and mix well to incorporate. Remove from the heat. Spoon the polenta into serving bowls and top with the hazelnuts and cauliflower. Garnish with the parsley and serve immediately.

SEEDED BEETROOT AND BUCKWHEAT BURGERS

These hearty and earthy vegetarian burgers combine the sweetness of beetroot and the nutty texture of seeds with wholesome buckwheat. You won't miss the meat with these!

SERVES 4 · PREP 15 MINS, PLUS SOAKING AND CHILLING · COOK 30 MINS

60g (2oz) uncooked buckwheat

125g (4½oz) beetroot, unpeeled and roughly chopped

85g (3oz) carrot, unpeeled and roughly chopped

30g (1oz) spring onions, trimmed and finely chopped

2 eggs

60g (2oz) oatmeal

½ tsp salt

60g (2oz) sunflower seeds

2–3 tbsp vegetable oil

1 Place the buckwheat in a large bowl and cover with water. Cover the bowl with a kitchen towel and leave to soak for at least 8 hours or for up to 12 hours. Then drain and rinse under running water.

2 Place the beetroot, carrots, and onions in a food processor and pulse for 1–2 minutes to combine. Then add the buckwheat, eggs, oatmeal, and salt and pulse until just incorporated.

3 Add 50g (1¾oz) of the sunflower seeds to the mixture, pulse to combine, and transfer to a large bowl. Add the remaining sunflower seeds and stir to combine. Chill in the fridge for 30 minutes. Divide the mixture into 4 equal portions, then shape each portion into a 9cm (4in) wide and 2cm (¾in) thick burger patty.

4 Heat the oil in a non-stick frying pan over a medium-high heat. Add the patties, once the oil is hot, and fry for about 5 minutes on each side or until firm and lightly coloured. Do this in batches to avoid overcrowding the pan. Remove from the heat and drain on a plate lined with kitchen paper. Serve with burger buns, mayonnaise, chips, and a green salad.

GRAIN EXCHANGE

You could use the same quantity of either of these grains instead of the buckwheat. Soak them in water overnight, then cook in 200ml (7fl oz) of water, and drain well. Leave to cool before using in the same way as the buckwheat.

quinoa

farro

millet

why not try...

Use **pumpkin seeds** in place of the sunflower seeds.

TEX MEX BURRITOS

An easy-to-make vegetable and millet wrap that makes for a delightful toasty, cheesy dinner.

SERVES 4 · PREP 15 MINS · COOK 20 MINS

1 tbsp olive oil

1 garlic clove, crushed

1 jalapeño pepper, finely chopped

60ml (2fl oz) lime juice

175g (6oz) prepared millet (see p22)

200g can black beans

4 large tortillas

115g (4oz) freshly grated Cheddar cheese

1 avocado, pitted and sliced

150g (5½oz) salsa (see p43)

1 Preheat the oven to 190°C (375°F/Gas 5). Heat the oil in a frying pan over a medium heat. Add the garlic and jalapeños and cook for 2 minutes, stirring occasionally, until the garlic is softened.

2 Then stir in the lime juice, millet, and black beans. Mix to combine and cook for 7 minutes or until heated through. Remove from the heat.

3 Divide the mixture evenly between the tortillas and top with equal quantities of the cheese, avocado, and salsa. Wrap the tortillas over the filling to form burritos. Enclose each burrito in a sheet of foil and cook in the oven for 10 minutes. Serve immediately.

BULGUR WHEAT, CARROT, AND COURGETTE FRITTERS

These are great as a quick snack, or to accompany roast chicken or a burger.

SERVES 4 · PREP 10 MINS, PLUS COOLING · COOK 40 MINS

60g (2oz) uncooked bulgur wheat

1 courgette, grated

1 carrot, grated

5g (¼oz) flat-leaf parsley, roughly chopped

4 large eggs, lightly beaten

salt and freshly ground black pepper

2 tbsp light olive oil

1 Place the bulgur wheat in a pan, cover with 300ml (10fl oz) of water, and bring to the boil. Then reduce the heat to a simmer and cook for 20–30 minutes or until all the water has been absorbed and the bulgur wheat is soft. Remove from the heat and leave to cool for 15 minutes.

2 Place all the vegetables in a clean kitchen towel or muslin cloth and squeeze out as much water as possible. Then transfer to a bowl and add the parsley, bulgur wheat, and eggs. Season with salt and pepper and mix well to combine.

3 Heat the oil in a large, non-stick frying pan over a medium-high heat. Add heaped spoonfuls of the vegetable mixture and lightly spread them out so that each fritter is about 7.5cm (3in) in diameter and 1cm (½in) thick. Fry the fritters for 2–3 minutes on each side, until golden brown on the outside and cooked through. Do this in batches to avoid overcrowding the pan. Remove with a slotted spoon and place on a lined plate. Serve hot.

FREEKEH KOFTE
WITH A TAHINI LEMON SAUCE

Traditionally made with minced beef or lamb, these meatballs are very popular in the Middle East and across Asia. The use of freekeh turns this version of kofte into a perfect vegetarian meal.

SERVES 4 · PREP 15 MINS, PLUS COOLING AND CHILLING · COOK 45 MINS

200g (7oz) cracked freekeh

1 small onion, finely chopped

1 egg

2 tsp ground cumin

1 tsp ground coriander

3 tbsp roughly chopped mint

12g (½oz) flat-leaf parsley, roughly chopped

½ tsp salt

20g (¾oz) rolled oats

40g (1½oz) wholewheat flour, plus extra if needed

4 tbsp light olive oil

FOR THE SAUCE

4 tbsp tahini sesame paste

juice of 1 lemon

1 garlic clove, finely chopped

¼ tsp salt

2 tbsp roughly chopped flat-leaf parsley

1 Place the freekeh and 1 litre (1¾ pints) of water in a large, lidded saucepan. Bring to the boil, then reduce the heat to a simmer. Cook for 20 minutes or until all the water has been absorbed and the freekeh is thick and sticky in texture. Remove from the heat, drain any remaining water, and leave to cool.

2 Add the onions, egg, cumin, coriander, mint, parsley, salt, oats, and flour to the freekeh. Mix well to combine, and place in the fridge to chill for at least 30 minutes.

3 Meanwhile, for the sauce, place the tahini, lemon juice, garlic, salt, and parsley in a bowl. Add 4 tablespoons of water and mix well to make a smooth paste. Add more water if the sauce seems too thick. Set aside.

4 On a clean work surface, shape the freekeh mixture into small balls about 4cm (1½in) in diameter. Add more flour if the mixture seems too loose and is not sticking together.

5 Heat 2 tablespoons of the oil in a non-stick frying pan over a medium-high heat. Once the oil is hot, add the kofte to the pan and fry for 5–8 minutes, turning frequently, until well browned all over and crispy on the outside. Remove with a slotted spoon, place on a lined plate, and keep warm. Do this in batches to avoid overcrowding the pan. Serve hot with the tahini sauce.

lemon

AMARANTH BLACK BEAN BURGERS
WITH AVOCADO CREAM

These vegetarian burgers are more than a match for any meat alternative. With a great texture from the combination of black beans and chewy amaranth and a hint of chilli, they work perfectly with the cool avocado cream.

SERVES 6 · PREP 15 MINS, PLUS COOLING · COOK 45 MINS

60g (2oz) uncooked amaranth

400g can black beans, drained

1 small red onion, finely chopped

½ tsp garlic granules, or ¼ tsp garlic powder

½ tsp chilli flakes

10g (¼oz) rolled oats

¼ tsp salt

6 burger buns, to serve

handful of cherry tomatoes, thinly sliced

1 small red onion, sliced into rings

FOR THE AVOCADO CREAM

2 avocados

juice of 1 lemon

pinch of salt

1 Place the amaranth in a large saucepan and cover with 130ml (4¼fl oz) of water. Bring to the boil, then reduce to a simmer, and cook for 12 minutes or until all the water has been absorbed. Remove from the heat, drain any remaining water, and leave to cool slightly.

2 Preheat the oven to 200°C (400°F/Gas 6). Grease and line a baking tray with baking parchment. Transfer the amaranth to a large bowl. Add the beans, onions, garlic granules, and chilli flakes. Mix well, using the back of a fork to mash the ingredients together. Then add the rolled oats and salt to the mixture. Mix until well incorporated.

3 Divide the mixture into 6 equal portions and shape each one into a ball. Gently press down each ball to form a burger patty about 7.5cm (3in) in diameter. Place the burgers on the prepared baking tray and transfer to the oven. Bake for 30 minutes or until they are firm to the touch and crispy on the outside.

4 For the avocado cream, scoop out the flesh from the avocado and place in a food processor. Add the lemon juice and salt and pulse until smooth. Place the burgers in the buns and top with the avocado cream. Serve alongside the tomatoes and onions.

BEEF AND BARLEY BURGERS

Beef burgers, but with a wholegrain upgrade. Adding the cooked barley makes these beef burgers tender and moist with a great texture. ideal for your next barbecue!

MAKES 4 LARGE BURGERS · PREP 20 MiNS, PLUS COOLiNG AND CHiLLiNG · COOK 1 HR

50g (1¾oz) uncooked pearl barley

500g (1lb 2oz) lean minced beef

1 large egg

100g (3½oz) onions, finely chopped

1 tsp mixed dried Italian herbs

salt and freshly ground black pepper

1 tbsp light olive oil, plus extra for greasing

1 Rinse the barley under cold running water, drain, and place in a large saucepan. Cover with water and bring to a simmer. Cook the barley for 30 minutes or until tender. Then drain, rinse under running water, and drain well again. Set aside to cool.

2 Place the beef, egg, onions, and Italian herbs in a large bowl. Season with salt and pepper and mix well to combine. Add the cooled barley to the bowl and mix until evenly incorporated.

3 Lightly grease a plate. Form the mixture into 4 burger patties, each roughly 10cm (4in) in diameter and 2cm (¾in) thick. Place them on the greased plate and cover with cling film. Chill the patties for about 20 minutes to help them keep their shape on cooking.

4 Heat the oil in a large frying pan over a medium heat. Fry the burger patties for about 10 minutes on each side, until well browned and cooked through. Remove from the heat. Serve the burgers with a selection of buns and accompaniments.

GRAiN EXCHANGE

For a variation, try using the same amount of either of these grains instead of the barley and cook them in the same way.

spelt

farro

VEGGIE BURGER WITH SPELT

These vegetarian burgers get their intense flavour from the super-absorbent spelt. Roasting the vegetables before they are added to the burgers helps retain more of their flavour and keeps the unnecessary moisture out.

MAKES 6 PATTIES · PREP 15 MINS, PLUS OVERNIGHT SOAKING AND CHILLING · COOK 1 HR

40g (1½oz) uncooked spelt

140g (5oz) shiitake mushrooms, sliced

3 tsp tamari or low-sodium soy sauce

1 large beetroot, about 100g (3½oz), grated

2 large carrots, about 100g (3½oz), grated

400g can kidney beans, drained

salt and freshly ground black pepper

1–2 tbsp olive oil

50g (1¾oz) ground almonds

40g (1½oz) panko breadcrumbs

2 tbsp spicy Dijon mustard

2 tbsp mayonnaise

2 spring onions, sliced

2 garlic cloves, pressed

2 large eggs

115g (4oz) tempeh, crumbled

FOR SERVING

6 burger buns

1 avocado, pitted and sliced

1 large tomato, sliced into rounds

1 large red onion, sliced into rounds

1 Place the spelt in a bowl, cover with water, and leave to soak overnight. Then drain well and rinse under running water. Place the spelt in a lidded saucepan. Pour over 240ml (8fl oz) of water and bring to the boil. Then reduce the heat to a simmer, cover, and cook for 50 minutes. Remove from the heat and set aside to cool.

2 Preheat the oven to 220°C (425°F/Gas 7). Spread out the mushrooms on a lined baking sheet and toss with 2 teaspoons of the tamari sauce. Spread out the beetroots, carrots, and beans on a separate sheet. Season with salt and pepper and toss with the oil. Place the sheets in the oven and bake for about 15 minutes. Then remove from the heat and lightly toss the vegetables and mushrooms. Return to the oven, rotating the positions of the sheets. Bake for a further 10 minutes or until the vegetables and beans are crisp and the mushrooms have lost most of their moisture. Remove from the heat and leave to cool.

3 Place the ground almonds, breadcrumbs, cooled vegetables, and remaining tamari in a food processor and pulse until just combined. Add the mustard, mayonnaise, spring onions, garlic, and eggs to the mixture. Season to taste with pepper and pulse to combine. Then add the spelt and tempeh and pulse lightly until just mixed, but still retaining some texture. Transfer the mixture to a large bowl, cover, and chill in the fridge for about 1 hour.

4 Set the grill or griddle pan at its medium-low setting. Divide the mixture into 6 equal portions and form each into a 2.5cm (1in) thick patty. Grill the patties for about 5 minutes on each side, until crisp on the outside. Remove from the heat. Serve hot with burger buns, avocado, tomatoes, and onions.

QUINOA SALMON CAKES

A fresh take on fish cakes, the peppers and quinoa add a whole new dimension to this quick recipe. Serve these easy-to-make cakes with a light tossed salad for a delicious and filling meal.

SERVES 4 · PREP 10 MINS, PLUS CHILLING · COOK 20 MINS

2 x 213g can salmon, drained, flaked, and pin boned

100g (3½oz) prepared quinoa (see p24)

2 eggs, beaten

2 garlic cloves, crushed

grated zest of 1 lemon

40g (1½oz) green peppers, deseeded and finely chopped

1 tsp freshly ground black pepper

sea salt

2–3 tbsp olive oil

1 lemon, cut into wedges, to serve

1 Place the salmon, quinoa, eggs, garlic, lemon zest, green peppers, and black pepper in a large bowl. Season to taste with sea salt and mix well until fully incorporated.

2 Divide the mixture into eight equal-sized portions. Gently form each portion into a patty-like shape. Place the cakes on a plate and chill in the fridge for about 15 minutes.

3 Heat the oil in a large frying pan over a medium heat. Gently place the cakes in the pan and fry for 4 minutes on each side, until golden brown and cooked through. Do this in batches to avoid overcrowding the pan. Remove from the heat and serve hot with lemon wedges and a watercress salad.

GRAIN EXCHANGE

For a change, try replacing the quinoa with the same amount of prepared **millet** and cook in the same way.

why not try...

For a variation, add cooked **white crab meat** or **tuna** instead of the salmon and cook as given in the recipe.

LAMB AND TEFF MEATBALLS

These impressive meatballs are moist and full of flavour, due to the inclusion of cinnamon, nutmeg, and teff.

SERVES 4 · PREP 10 MINS, PLUS CHILLING · COOK 20 MINS

50g (1¾oz) teff flour	¼ tsp grated nutmeg
450g (1lb) minced lamb	¼ tsp ground cinnamon
2 spring onions, about 30g (1oz) in total, finely diced	salt and freshly ground black pepper
1 tsp ground cumin	1 egg, lightly beaten

1 Place the flour, lamb, onions, cumin, nutmeg, and cinnamon in a large bowl. Season with ½ teaspoon of salt and a good grinding of pepper. Mix well to combine. Then add the egg and mix until fully incorporated. Cover the bowl with cling film and place in the fridge for 30 minutes.

2 Preheat the oven to 180°C (350°F/Gas 4). Line a baking sheet with baking parchment. Divide the mixture into 12 equal portions and shape into balls. Place the meatballs on the baking sheet and bake in the oven for 10 minutes.

3 Remove from the heat and turn the meatballs over. Return to the oven and bake for a further 10 minutes. Remove from the oven and check the meatballs for doneness. They will be cooked to medium. If you prefer them well done, return the meatballs to the oven for a further 5 minutes. Remove from the heat and serve warm.

CHIPOTLE BLACK BEAN BURGERS

This quick and easy recipe combines wholegrains and spicy chipotle chillies to make the perfect burger patties.

MAKES 6 · PREP 10 MINS · COOK 20 MINS

400g can black beans, drained and rinsed	90g (3¼oz) rolled oats
1 small onion, quartered	1 large egg
2 cloves garlic	½ avocado, pitted and thinly sliced
2 chipotle peppers in 1 tsp adobo sauce	1 large tomato, sliced into rounds
½ tsp salt	
175g (6oz) prepared bulgur wheat (see p22)	

1 Preheat the oven to 190°C (375°F/Gas 5). Place the black beans, onions, garlic, chipotle peppers, and adobo sauce in a food processor. Pulse until well combined. Transfer the mixture to a bowl.

2 Lightly grease a baking sheet and set aside. Add the salt, bulgur wheat, rolled oats, and egg to the bowl. Mix well until evenly combined. Divide the mixture into six equal portions and form each into a burger patty. Place the patties in the baking sheet and place in the oven.

3 Bake for 10–12 minutes, then remove from the oven. Turn the patties over and return to the oven for a further 10 minutes, until browned and cooked through. Remove from the heat. Serve immediately with burger buns and avocado, tomatoes, and lettuce.

BAKED FREEKEH ARANCINI

Arancini balls are typically made from leftover risotto. This recipe recreates this tasty italian treat with freekeh and a unique mozzarella and pine nut filling for a healthier and nuttier dish.

MAKES 12 · PREP 15 MINS, PLUS CHILLING · COOK 50 MINS

175g (6oz) cracked freekeh

600ml (1 pint) chicken stock

85g (3oz) freshly grated mozzarella cheese

2 tbsp pine nuts, lightly toasted and finely chopped

1 tbsp finely chopped flat-leaf parsley

salt and freshly ground black pepper

2 large eggs, lightly beaten

30g (1oz) freshly grated Parmesan cheese

85g (3oz) panko breadcrumbs

2 tbsp sunflower oil

marinara sauce, to serve

1 Place the freekeh and stock in a large saucepan and bring to the boil. Reduce the heat to a simmer and cook for 25 minutes. Remove from the heat and drain any remaining water. Spread out the freekeh on a large plate and leave to cool completely. Then place in the fridge to chill.

2 Preheat the oven to 220°C (425°F/Gas 7). Line a baking sheet with baking parchment and set aside. Place the mozzarella, pine nuts, and parsley in a bowl. Add a pinch of salt, season to taste with pepper, and mix well to combine. In a separate bowl, place the eggs, Parmesan, and 60g (2oz) of the breadcrumbs. Add the freekeh and mix well to combine. Place the remaining breadcrumbs in a shallow dish.

3 Divide the freekeh mixture into 12 equal parts and form into balls. Use your finger to press through the middle of each ball to form a hole. Fill these with the mozzarella mixture and pinch the sides together to seal. Brush the balls with the oil, then lightly toss through the breadcrumbs to coat.

4 Place the balls on the prepared baking sheet, transfer to the oven, and bake for 20–25 minutes, until golden brown. Then remove from the heat and serve warm with marinara sauce. These can be stored for up to 1 day in the fridge.

POLENTA WiTH TOMATO, MOZZARELLA, PARMA HAM, AND PESTO

As a healthy alternative to fried bread, polenta is the perfect foundation for this light lunch or supper dish. The salty Parma ham is complemented by the creamy mozzarella, with the pesto adding a hint of warm italian summers.

SERVES 4 · PREP 15 MiNS · COOK 10 MiNS

1 tbsp light olive oil

8 x 1cm (½in) thick slices of baked polenta (see p25) or precooked, shop-bought polenta, about 300g (10oz) in total

2 tomatoes, cut into 8 slices

8 x 1cm (½in) thick slices mozzarella cheese, about 300g (10oz) in total

8 slices Parma ham

85g (3oz) ready-made basil pesto (or see p62 for step-by-step instructions)

1 Heat the oil in a large frying pan set over a medium heat. Add the polenta and fry for about 5 minutes on each side, until golden brown. Remove from the pan.

2 Divide the polenta slices between four plates. Top each one with a slice of tomato and mozzarella. Place a slice of ham on each stack and drizzle evenly with the pesto. Serve immediately.

basil

BEEF AND BULGUR WHEAT MEATBALLS
WITH CREAMY PESTO SAUCE

This dish brings together flavoursome and wholesome meatballs with a delightful sauce made from traditional pesto mixed with whipping cream. It's the perfect recipe for a delicious dinner.

SERVES 4 · PREP 10 MINS · COOK 35 MINS

450g (1lb) minced beef

60g (2oz) fresh breadcrumbs, seasoned with salt and pepper

60g (2oz) prepared bulgur wheat (see p22)

2 large eggs

1 tbsp pesto (see p63)

½ tsp salt

¼ tsp pepper

FOR THE SAUCE

1 tbsp butter

1 tbsp plain flour

225ml tub whipping cream

225g (8oz) pesto

1 Preheat the oven to 190°C (375°F/Gas 5). Lightly grease a baking sheet and set aside. Place the beef, breadcrumbs, bulgur wheat, eggs, and pesto in a large bowl. Season with the salt and pepper. Mix until thoroughly combined.

2 Form the mixture into 12 balls and arrange on the prepared baking sheet. Bake the meatballs for 15 minutes, then remove from the oven and flip them over. Return the meatballs to the oven and bake for a further 10 minutes, until cooked through.

3 Meanwhile, for the sauce, melt the butter in a saucepan. Add the flour and cook, whisking constantly, until it turns a pale golden colour. Then add the cream, a little at a time, and whisk constantly until fully incorporated.

4 Add the pesto and whisk until thoroughly combined. Season to taste if needed, and mix well to combine. Serve the meatballs hot with the sauce poured over.

BAKED BUTTERNUT SQUASH FRITTERS

These appealing and healthy fritters are baked instead of fried. The amaranth flour brings a slightly nutty note to the dish and the polenta adds the crispness usually attained from deep-frying.

MAKES 10 FRITTERS · PREP 15 MINS, PLUS COOLING · COOK 1 HR 15 MINS

1 small butternut squash, about 300g (10oz)

60g (2oz) amaranth flour

1 garlic clove, pressed

2 tbsp roughly chopped chives

½ tsp ground cumin

¼ tsp cayenne pepper

salt and freshly ground black pepper

1 tbsp extra virgin olive oil

1 tbsp maple syrup

50g (1¾oz) freshly grated Parmesan cheese

75g (2½oz) polenta

1 Preheat the oven to 200°C (400°F/Gas 6). Use a fork to poke holes in the butternut squash, then place it in a roasting tin. Place the tin in the oven and roast for about 45 minutes, until soft. Remove from the heat and leave to cool slightly. Reduce the temperature to 180°C (350°F/Gas 4). Line a baking sheet with baking parchment and set aside.

2 Once cooled, cut the squash in half and remove the seeds. Scoop out all the flesh and place in a large bowl. Use the back of a fork to mash the squash until smooth. Then add the amaranth, garlic, chives, cumin, and cayenne pepper. Season with a pinch of salt and a good grinding of black pepper. Stir to combine. Pour in the oil and maple syrup. Sprinkle over the cheese and mix well to combine.

3 Place the polenta in a shallow dish. Take spoonfuls of the squash mixture, form into balls, and toss in the polenta to coat. Lay the balls on the prepared baking sheet and flatten slightly. Bake the fritters for 25–30 minutes or until golden brown and cooked through. Serve warm.

chives

SAUSAGE AND FARRO STUFFED PORTABELLA MUSHROOMS

Mild sausages are combined with earthy farro and roasted mushrooms in this wonderfully textured dish. Serve them on their own as a starter or pair with a tossed salad for a light dinner.

SERVES 4 · PREP 15 MiNS · COOK 40 MiNS

150g (5½oz) sweet Italian sausages

1 tbsp olive oil

1 small onion, finely diced

1 green pepper, deseeded and finely diced

4 large portabella mushroom caps, stems reserved and finely chopped

100g (3½oz) prepared farro (see p22)

1 large egg, lightly beaten

1 tsp smoked paprika

salt and freshly ground black pepper

1 Preheat the oven to 190°C (375°F/Gas 5). Heat a small frying pan over a medium heat. Add the sausages and cook for 5–10 minutes or until well browned and cooked through. Remove from the heat and leave to cool slightly before chopping into bite-sized pieces.

2 Heat the oil in a frying pan over a medium heat. Add the onions, green peppers, and mushroom stems. Cook for about 10 minutes, stirring occasionally, until lightly browned. Transfer to a large bowl, add the sausages and farro, and mix to combine. Then add the egg and smoked paprika and season to taste. Stir well to combine.

3 Use a spoon to scrape out and discard the ribs from the mushroom caps. Divide the sausage and farro mixture evenly between the mushroom caps and press down lightly to set. Place on a baking sheet and bake for about 20 minutes or until the caps have softened and the filling has cooked through. Remove from the oven and leave to cool slightly. Serve warm.

POLENTA FRIES WITH ROSEMARY AND GARLIC

Far healthier than anything served by your local chip shop, these polenta fries are boosted in flavour thanks to the rosemary and garlic. Pair them with a spelt veggie burger for the perfect wholegrain meal.

SERVES 4–6 · PREP 15 MINS, PLUS CHILLING · COOK 30 MINS

1–2 tbsp olive oil, plus extra for greasing

750ml (1¼ pints) chicken stock

1 tbsp butter

150g (5½oz) quick-cook polenta

1 garlic clove, pressed

1 tbsp finely chopped rosemary

salt and freshly ground black pepper

1 Grease a baking sheet and set aside. Place the stock and butter in a saucepan and bring to the boil. Then reduce the heat to medium-low and gradually add the polenta, whisking constantly. Cook for about 2 minutes, whisking constantly, until all the liquid has been absorbed and the polenta has thickened and is smooth.

2 Remove from the heat, add the garlic and rosemary, and mix well to combine. Transfer the polenta mixture to the baking sheet and spread it out to form an even 1cm (½in) thick layer. Place the baking sheet in the refrigerator to chill for 3 hours.

3 Preheat the oven to 200°C (400°F/Gas 6). Grease another baking sheet and set aside. Place the polenta on a clean surface and slice into long rectangular pieces. Spread out the fries on the prepared baking sheet and lightly brush with oil. Season well and bake for 20–25 minutes or until they are golden brown at the edges. Remove from the heat and serve immediately.

SPICY QUINOA AND KAMUT CAKES
WITH A MANGO HABANERO SAUCE

These tasty and versatile cakes can be served as fun appetisers or finger food and will tingle the taste-buds with their deceptive spiciness. Dip them in the mango habanero sauce for a fiery yet fruity flavour.

MAKES 12 SMALL CAKES · PREP 20 MINS, PLUS OVERNIGHT SOAKING AND CHILLING · COOK 1 HR 10 MINS

85g (3oz) uncooked kamut, soaked overnight

salt and freshly ground black pepper

85g (3oz) uncooked quinoa

2–4 tbsp grapeseed oil, plus extra if needed

3 eggs, lightly beaten

8 tbsp mustard greens, finely chopped

handful of coriander leaves, finely chopped

1 jalapeño, deseeded and finely chopped

3 shallots, finely chopped

3 garlic cloves, pressed

1 tsp ground cumin

½ tsp baking powder

60g (2oz) chickpea flour

FOR THE SAUCE

1 tbsp grapeseed oil

1 large, ripe mango, pitted and diced

1 small habanero chilli, deseeded and diced

1 garlic clove, crushed

1 shallot, roughly chopped

2 tbsp white wine vinegar

1 Place the kamut in a saucepan and cover with 375ml (13fl oz) of water. Add a pinch of salt and bring to the boil. Then reduce the heat to a simmer, cover, and cook for about 40 minutes. Then remove from the heat, drain any remaining water, and spread out on a baking sheet to cool.

2 Meanwhile, place the quinoa in a separate saucepan and cover with 250ml (9fl oz) of water. Add a pinch of salt and bring to the boil. Then reduce the heat to a simmer, cover, and cook for 10–15 minutes or until almost all the water has been absorbed. Then remove from the heat and drain any remaining water. Transfer to the baking sheet with the kamut and leave to cool to room temperature, then chill in the fridge for 10–15 minutes.

3 For the sauce, heat the oil in a frying pan over a medium heat. Add the mango, habanero chilli, garlic, shallots, and vinegar. Cook for 10 minutes, stirring frequently, until the mango has softened and broken down. Transfer the mixture to a food processor and pulse until smooth. Place the sauce in a bowl and set aside to cool.

4 Preheat the oven to 180°C (350°F/Gas 4). Place the kamut, quinoa, eggs, mustard greens, coriander, jalapeños, shallots, garlic, and cumin in a large bowl. Season with ½ teaspoon of salt and a good grinding of pepper and mix well to combine. Then add the baking powder and flour and mix until well combined. Chill in the fridge for 20–25 minutes.

5 Line a baking sheet with baking parchment. Divide the mixture into 12 equal portions and form each into a ball. Flatten the balls slightly to make patties that are about 5cm (2in) in diameter. Place the patties on the prepared baking sheet. Bake for about 10 minutes. Remove from the heat.

6 Heat the oil in a frying pan over a medium heat. Once the oil is hot, place the cakes in the pan and cook for 2–3 minutes on each side, until browned. Do this in batches to avoid overcrowding the pan. Remove from the heat and serve warm with the sauce.

HEARTY STEWS AND BAKED DISHES

KITCHARI STEW WITH KAMUT

The word "kitchari" literally means mixture, and is an Indian recipe that mixes two or more grains for a soothing and warming dish. This recipe uses kamut instead of rice, for more texture and bite.

SERVES 3 · PREP 10 MINS, PLUS OVERNIGHT SOAKING · COOK 2 HRS 10 MINS

150g (5½oz) yellow split peas

100g (3½oz) uncooked kamut

1 tbsp coconut oil or ghee

5cm (2in) piece of fresh root ginger, finely chopped

2 tsp turmeric

2 tsp ground cumin

1 tsp ground coriander

½ tsp ground cinnamon

salt

handful of coriander leaves, to garnish

1 Place the peas in a large bowl, cover with water, and leave to soak for about 12 hours. Place the kamut in a separate bowl, cover with water, and leave to soak overnight or for up to 8 hours. Drain any remaining water from the peas and kamut. Rinse under running water, drain well, and set aside.

2 Heat the oil in a large, lidded saucepan over a medium heat. Add the ginger, turmeric, cumin, coriander, and cinnamon. Reduce the heat to low and cook for 1–2 minutes, stirring frequently, making sure the spices do not burn.

3 Add the peas, kamut, and 1.5 litres (2¾ pints) of water to the pan. Season with salt and bring the mixture to a simmer. Cover partially and cook, stirring occasionally, for 2 hours or until the peas have broken down and the kamut is tender and chewy. Taste and adjust the seasoning, if needed. Remove from the heat and garnish with coriander. Serve hot.

GRAIN EXCHANGE

For a change, use the same amount of either of the following grains in place of the kamut.

spelt

wheat berries

BAKED MOROCCAN LAMB STEW WITH FREEKEH

Easy to prepare, slow cooking this dish in the oven brings about a warming combination of tenderness from the lamb and a rich and creamy texture from the freekeh. The dried fruit adds something special to every bite.

SERVES 2–3 · PREP 10 MINS · COOK 2 HRS

1 tbsp light olive oil

350g (12oz) boneless lamb shoulder, diced

100g (3½oz) uncooked freekeh

400g can chopped tomatoes

2 tbsp ground cumin

¼ tsp grated fresh root ginger

½ tsp ground cinnamon

¼ tsp salt

100g (3½oz) dried apricots, roughly chopped

3 tbsp chopped coriander

1 Preheat the oven to 180°C (350°F/Gas 4). Heat the oil in a large, lidded flameproof dish over a medium heat. Add the lamb and cook for about 5 minutes, stirring occasionally, until lightly browned all over. Remove from the heat.

2 Add the freekeh, tomatoes, cumin, ginger, cinnamon, and salt to the lamb and stir well. Then add 250ml (9fl oz) of water and mix to combine. Cover, transfer to the oven, and bake for about 45 minutes.

3 Remove from the oven. Add the apricots to the dish, stir well, and return to the oven. Cook for another hour or until the freekeh is tender and chewy and the lamb is cooked through. Remove from the heat and transfer to a large serving dish. Garnish with coriander and serve hot.

GRAIN EXCHANGE

This dish works really well with quinoa and millet, too. Use the same amount of grain as the freekeh, reduce the water quantity to 200ml (7fl oz) for both grains, and cook as above.

quinoa

millet

SHORT RIB STEW OVER POLENTA

A great comfort food for a cold day, this stew is served over polenta, which adds a little more richness to this dish. The braised ribs are deliciously tender and will fill your home with the most wonderful aromas.

SERVES 4–6 · PREP 10 MINS · COOK 3 HRS 25 MINS

2 tbsp plain flour

salt and freshly ground black pepper

3 tbsp sunflower oil

1.35kg (3lb) boneless short ribs

500ml (16fl oz) good-quality red wine, such as Cabernet

600ml (1 pint) beef stock

1 onion, diced

3 garlic cloves, crushed and sliced, plus 1 garlic clove, crushed

4 carrots, diced

3 red potatoes, diced

70g (2¼oz) chestnut or baby portobella mushrooms, sliced

1 tsp dried thyme

½ tsp dried rosemary

½ tsp dried sage

500ml (16fl oz) milk

175g (6oz) quick-cook polenta

handful of fresh thyme sprigs, to garnish

handful of mustard cress, to garnish

1 Place the flour in a shallow dish. Season the short ribs and toss in the flour to coat. Heat the oil in a Dutch oven or large casserole, over a medium-high heat. Add the short ribs and cook for 5–6 minutes, until lightly coloured on all sides. Then add the wine and bring to the boil. Cook for about 10 minutes or until the liquid has been reduced by half.

2 Add the stock and bring to the boil. Then reduce the heat to low, cover, and simmer for 2–2 ½ hours or until the meat is tender. Check the stew occasionally and skim away any fat from the surface.

3 Add the onions, garlic, carrots, potatoes, and mushrooms and stir to mix. Then add the thyme, rosemary, and sage. Season with ½ teaspoon of salt and pepper. Cook the stew for a further 40 minutes, until the vegetables are soft and cooked through.

4 Meanwhile, place the milk in a saucepan and season with pepper and ¼ teaspoon of salt. Add 240ml (8fl oz) of water and bring to the boil. Add the polenta, a little at a time, stirring constantly. Reduce the heat to low and cook for 2 minutes, stirring constantly, until the polenta is cooked and pulling away from the sides. Add the garlic, season to taste, and mix well. Spoon the polenta into bowls, ladle over the stew, and garnish with thyme and mustard cress. Serve hot.

RATATOUILLE CASSEROLE WITH FARRO AND FETA

A mix of baked Mediterranean vegetables, tomato sauce, and tender farro is topped with contrasting salty feta cheese for a warm and filling meal that is perfect at any time of the year.

SERVES 4 · PREP 10 MINS, PLUS OVERNIGHT SOAKING · COOK 1 HR 30 MINS

100g (3½oz) uncooked farro

1 aubergine, cut into cubes

½ tsp salt

2 red or orange peppers, deseeded and cut into bite-sized pieces

1 courgette, cut into bite-sized pieces

1 red onion, finely chopped

1 tbsp light olive oil

400g can chopped tomatoes

250ml (9fl oz) vegetable stock

¼ tsp dried rosemary

1 garlic clove, finely chopped

200g (7oz) feta cheese, crumbled

2 tsp chopped basil leaves, to serve

1 Place the farro in a large bowl, cover with water, and leave to soak overnight or for up to 8 hours. Then drain any remaining water, rinse under running water, and drain well again. Set aside.

2 Preheat the oven to 180°C (350°F/Gas 4). Place the aubergine cubes in a colander, sprinkle with the salt, and press down with a heavy object. Leave to draw out the water and any bitterness.

3 Place the peppers, courgette, onions, and aubergine in a 2 litre (3½ pint) casserole. Spread them out evenly and drizzle with the oil. Add the farro to the dish and toss lightly to mix with the vegetables.

4 Place the tomatoes, stock, rosemary, and garlic in a large bowl and mix to combine. Add the mixture to the casserole and mix well. Cover, place in the oven, and bake for 1 hour and 15 minutes or until the vegetables are tender and the farro is cooked.

5 Remove from the heat, take off the lid, and sprinkle over the feta. Return to the oven, uncovered, and cook for about 15 minutes or until the feta starts to turn golden. Remove from the heat and season to taste if needed. Garnish with basil and serve hot.

BEEF AND SPELT STEW

This dish is ideal for when you just want to leave something to cook in the oven while you are busy with other things. Adding spelt to this traditional beef stew provides an extra nutty and chewy texture.

SERVES 4 · PREP 15 MINS, PLUS OVERNIGHT SOAKING · COOK 2 HRS 45 MINS

150g (5½oz) uncooked spelt

2 tbsp light olive oil

1 onion, finely chopped

2 celery sticks, finely chopped

2 garlic cloves, finely chopped

500g (1lb 2oz) stewing beef steak, diced

2 carrots, chopped into bite-sized pieces

150g (5½oz) mushrooms, sliced

400g can chopped tomatoes

750ml (1¼ pints) beef stock

1 tsp dried sage

1 tsp dried thyme

salt and freshly ground black pepper

1 Place the spelt in a bowl, cover with plenty of water, and leave to soak overnight or for up to 8 hours. Then drain and rinse under running cold water. Drain well again and set aside.

2 Preheat the oven to 160°C (320°F/Gas 3). Heat the oil in a frying pan over a medium-high heat. Add the onions, celery, and garlic and sauté for about 3 minutes. Then add the beef and cook for 8–10 minutes, stirring frequently, until well browned all over. Remove from the heat.

3 Transfer the beef and onion mixture, along with any juices, to a 3 litre (5¼ pint) heavy-based ovenproof casserole. Then add the carrots, mushrooms, tomatoes, stock, dried herbs, and spelt. Mix well to combine, cover, and place in the oven.

4 Cook the stew for 2½ hours or until the beef is cooked through and the vegetables and spelt are tender. Remove from the heat. Taste, adjusting the seasoning if needed, and serve hot.

carrots

BAKED CHICKEN FREEKEH PAELLA

This easy one-pot dish works as a simple weekday supper and is impressive enough to serve when entertaining, too.

SERVES 4 · PREP 15 MINS · COOK 45 MINS

4 chicken legs, about 1.35kg (3lb) in total	2 red peppers, deseeded and thinly sliced
salt and freshly ground black pepper	1 red chilli, deseeded and thinly sliced
¼ tsp smoked paprika	1 onion, thinly sliced
¼ tsp chilli flakes	5 garlic cloves, smashed and sliced
250g (9oz) uncooked freekeh	juice of ½ a lemon
400ml (14fl oz) chicken stock	1 tbsp roughly chopped flat-leaf parsley, to garnish
120ml (4fl oz) dry white wine	
175g (6oz) chorizo sausage	

1 Preheat the oven to 190°C (375°F/Gas 5). Place the chicken legs, skin-side up, on a clean work surface and season generously with salt and pepper. Then rub evenly with the smoked paprika and chilli flakes.

2 Place the freekeh, stock, and wine in a large ovenproof casserole. Then add the chorizo, red peppers, red chillies, onions, and garlic and place the chicken on top. Cover and transfer the casserole to the oven.

3 Roast for 35 minutes. Then remove the lid and roast for a further 10 minutes, until the chicken is cooked through and golden, the freekeh is fluffy, and almost all the liquid has been absorbed. Remove from the heat and drizzle over the lemon juice. Garnish with the parsley and serve hot.

CHEESY CHICKEN AND BROCCOLI CASSEROLE WITH BULGUR WHEAT

Chicken and a creamy cheese sauce combine with bulgur wheat for a comforting casserole.

SERVES 4 · PREP 20 MINS, PLUS COOLING · COOK 30 MINS

40g (1½oz) unsalted butter	200g (7oz) prepared bulgur wheat (see p22)
20g (¾oz) plain flour	225g (8oz) cooked chicken breast, diced
750ml (1¼ pints) milk	1 small broccoli, cut into florets and steamed
2 tsp mustard powder	
salt and freshly ground black pepper	60g (2oz) shredded smoked Gouda cheese
225g (8oz) grated mature Cheddar cheese	

1 Preheat the oven to 190°C (375°F/Gas 5). Melt the butter in a saucepan over a medium heat. Whisk in the flour and cook for about 3 minutes or until golden. Then add the milk and whisk until well combined. Bring to the boil and simmer, whisking constantly, for 5 minutes or until slightly thickened.

2 Remove from the heat and add the mustard. Season to taste and mix well to combine. Add the Cheddar, a little at a time, whisking until fully melted and incorporated. Then add the bulgur wheat, chicken, and broccoli. Mix well to combine.

3 Transfer the bulgur wheat and broccoli mixture to an ovenproof dish and spread out to form an even layer. Sprinkle over the Gouda. Bake for 15–20 minutes or until bubbly at the edges. Remove from the heat and leave to cool slightly. Serve warm.

THAI GREEN CHICKEN AND MILLET CURRY
WITH WINTER SQUASH

An easy and quick one-pot meal, in this recipe a creamy Thai curry of tender chicken and sweet baked butternut squash is enhanced by the addition of fluffy millet and is perfect for a wholesome lunch or dinner.

SERVES 4 · PREP 15–20 MINS · COOK 40 MINS

1 tbsp coconut oil or light olive oil

4 tbsp Thai green curry paste

5cm (2in) piece of fresh root ginger

400g (14oz) boneless chicken thighs, diced

400ml can coconut milk

600ml (1 pint) chicken stock

1 small butternut squash, deseeded and cut into bite-sized pieces

200g (7oz) uncooked millet

handful of coriander leaves, to garnish

1 Heat the oil in a large, lidded saucepan over a medium-high heat. Add the curry paste and ginger and cook for about 1 minute, stirring frequently. Then add the chicken and cook for a further 5 minutes, stirring frequently, until lightly browned.

2 Add the coconut milk, stock, squash, and millet to the pan. Stir to mix and reduce the heat to a simmer. Cover and cook for a further 30 minutes or until the chicken is cooked through and the millet and squash are tender. Taste and adjust the seasoning if needed. Remove from the heat. Garnish with coriander and serve hot.

GRAIN EXCHANGE

This dish also works well with **quinoa**. Use the same quantity of grain as the millet and cook in the same way.

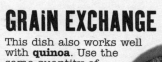

why not try...

You could try adding a small **kabocha squash** in place of the butternut squash, or garnish with **rocket** instead of the coriander.

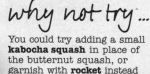

SPiCY GARLiC QUiNOA WiTH SEAFOOD STEW

This seafood stew is deceptively simple to make and very satisfying. You can play around with different seafood combinations, trying out varieties that are local, seasonal, and sustainable.

SERVES 4 · PREP 15 MiNS, PLUS COOLING · COOK 55 MiNS

175g (6oz) uncooked quinoa

pinch of salt

5 tbsp extra virgin olive oil

1 onion, thinly sliced

1 fennel bulb, thinly sliced and fronds reserved

1 large potato, diced into 1cm (½ in) cubes

6 garlic cloves, thinly sliced

175g (6oz) chorizo sausage, diced

120ml (4fl oz) dry white wine

1 tbsp tomato purée

pinch of saffron

400g can chopped tomatoes

750ml (1¼ pints) chicken stock

¼ tsp chilli flakes

1 tsp lemon juice, plus extra to serve

1 tsp grated zest of lemon

350g (12oz) firm white fish, such as halibut, diced

225g (8oz) uncooked prawns, peeled and deveined

225g (8oz) clams

225g (8oz) mussels

handful of flat-leaf parsley

1 Rinse the quinoa under running water and place in a large saucepan. Cover with 500ml (16fl oz) of water, season with a pinch of salt, and bring to the boil. Reduce the heat to a simmer and cook for about 15 minutes, until tender. Then remove from the heat, drain any remaining water, and leave to cool slightly.

2 For the stew, heat 3 tablespoons of the oil in a large, heavy-based saucepan over a medium heat. Add the onions, fennel, and potatoes. Cook for about 10 minutes, stirring frequently, until the onions and fennel have softened and are starting to brown. Then add half the garlic and cook for a further 2 minutes.

3 Add the chorizo and cook for 3 minutes, stirring frequently, until browned. Then add the wine and cook until reduced. Add the tomato purée and saffron and stir to combine. Add the tomatoes and stock and bring to the boil. Then reduce the heat to a simmer and cook for about 20 minutes, or until the liquid has reduced and the potatoes are soft.

4 Meanwhile, heat the remaining oil in a large frying pan over a medium-low heat. Add the chilli flakes and the remaining garlic. Cook for about 2 minutes, stirring frequently, until the garlic is fragrant. Add the cooled quinoa and stir to coat with the oil. Remove from the heat, drizzle over the lemon juice, and toss to combine. Set aside and keep warm.

5 Once the potatoes are cooked through, add the lemon zest and fish to the stew, and cook for a further 2–3 minutes. Then add the prawns, clams, and mussels. Cover and cook until the prawns are cooked and the mussels and clams are open. Remove from the heat. Take out and discard any mussels and clams that did not open. Place the quinoa in a large serving bowl, top with the seafood stew, and drizzle over some lemon juice. Roughly chop the parsley and sprinkle over the stew. Serve immediately.

THAI YELLOW PUMPKIN CURRY WITH MILLET

Perfect for vegans, this vibrant curry with its fresh, Thai flavours uses pumpkin and millet to create a hearty and warming supper that is really comforting in the autumn or winter.

SERVES 4–6 · PREP 10 MINS · COOK 40 MINS

1 tbsp coconut oil
  or sunflower oil

3 tbsp Thai yellow curry paste

1 onion, finely chopped

1 pumpkin, about 800g (1¾lb),
  deseeded and chopped into
  bite-sized pieces

400ml can coconut milk

300ml (10fl oz) vegetable stock

200g (7oz) uncooked millet

400g can chickpeas, drained

salt and freshly ground
  black pepper

4 tbsp chopped coriander
  leaves, to garnish

2 limes, cut into wedges

1 Heat the oil in a large, lidded saucepan over a medium heat. Add the curry paste and onions and cook for 2 minutes, stirring frequently. Then add the pumpkin, coconut milk, stock, and millet to the pan. Bring to a simmer, cover, and cook for about 30 minutes.

2 Add the chickpeas and cook for 5 minutes or until the pumpkin is tender. Taste and adjust the seasoning as necessary. Remove from the heat. Garnish with coriander and serve immediately with lime wedges.

GRAIN EXCHANGE

For a variation, you could use the same amount of **quinoa** in place of the millet.

why not try...

You could try using **butternut squash** in place of the pumpkin, and garnish with **flat-leaf parsley** instead of the coriander.

SPICY CHICKEN AND SORGHUM STEW

This delicious, warming stew makes excellent use of leftover roast chicken and is spiced with the inclusion of chorizo sausage. The depth of flavours will vary, based on the use of chorizo made from fresh or smoked pork.

SERVES 4 · PREP 15 MINS · COOK 1 HR 40 MINS

100g (3½oz) uncooked sorghum

salt and freshly ground black pepper

3 tbsp sunflower oil

175g (6oz) chorizo sausage, diced

1 onion, diced

3 hot red cherry peppers, deseeded and diced

2 celery sticks, diced

2 carrots, diced

3 garlic cloves, crushed and roughly chopped

1 tbsp tomato purée

3 tbsp plain flour

1 litre (1¾ pints) chicken stock

1 bay leaf

450g (1lb) roasted chicken, shredded

2 spring onions, thinly sliced

1 tbsp roughly chopped flat-leaf parsley

1 Place the sorghum in a lidded saucepan and cover with 750ml (1¼ pints) of water. Add a pinch of salt, stir to mix, and bring to the boil. Then reduce the heat to a simmer, cover, and cook for 45 minutes or until almost all of the water has been absorbed. Remove from the heat and leave, covered, for about 10 minutes. Then drain any remaining water and set aside.

2 Meanwhile, heat the oil in a large soup pot over a medium heat. Add the chorizo and cook, stirring frequently, for 2–3 minutes or until lightly browned. Then add the onions, red cherry peppers, celery, and carrots. Cook for 8–10 minutes, stirring frequently, until the vegetables have softened.

3 Add in the garlic and tomato purée and cook, stirring frequently, for 2 minutes. Then season with ½ teaspoon of salt and a good grinding of pepper. Add the flour, stir well, and cook for 2–3 minutes, stirring constantly.

4 Pour in the stock and add the bay leaf. Bring to the boil, then reduce the heat to a simmer, and cook for a further 10 minutes. Then remove the bay leaf. Add the chicken and sorghum and stir to mix. Cook the stew for 20–30 minutes, until thickened. Remove from the heat. Garnish with spring onions and parsley and serve hot.

SUMMER BEAN STEW WITH WHEAT BERRIES

Great as a filling lunch or light dinner, this stew is packed with hearty beans and sweet wheat berries. Delicious eaten on its own, this dish can also be served with grilled meats, such as lamb chops.

SERVES 4 · PREP 15 MINS, PLUS OVERNIGHT SOAKING · COOK 55 MINS

- 100g (3½oz) uncooked wheat berries
- 1 tbsp light olive oil
- 1 onion, finely chopped
- 2 garlic cloves, finely chopped
- 2 celery sticks, finely chopped
- 2 yellow or red peppers, deseeded and diced
- 1 courgette, diced
- 500ml (16fl oz) vegetable stock
- 400g can haricot beans, drained
- 400g can borlotti beans, drained
- 400g can chopped tomatoes
- 2 tsp Italian herb seasoning
- salt and freshly ground black pepper
- handful of basil leaves, to garnish

1 Place the wheat berries in a large bowl and cover with water. Leave to soak overnight or for at least 8 hours. Then drain any remaining water and rinse under running water. Drain well and set aside.

2 Heat the oil in a large soup pot over a medium heat. Add the onions and garlic and sauté for about 3 minutes or until the onions are translucent. Add the celery and sauté for a further 2 minutes. Then add the peppers and courgette and cook for 3 minutes, stirring frequently.

3 Add the stock, wheat berries, both lots of beans, tomatoes, and Italian seasoning. Stir well and reduce the heat to a simmer. Cover and cook for 45 minutes, until the vegetables and wheat berries are tender. Season to taste, if needed, and remove from the heat. Serve hot, garnished with basil.

GRAIN EXCHANGE

This dish works well with a variety of similar grains. Use the same amount of any of the following grains and cook them in the same way as the wheat berries.

kamut

spelt

farro

why not try...

Try using 4–6 **runner beans** instead of the courgette or peppers, and a small handful of **pea shoots**, to garnish, instead of the basil.

COWBOY QUINOA CHILLI

This modern take on an American classic is packed with the flavours of Tex-mex cuisine and the nutty texture of quinoa. Easy to prepare, this chilli provides a rich and satisfying meal.

SERVES 4–6 · PREP 15 MINS · COOK 1 HR 10 MINS

1 tbsp light olive oil

1 onion, finely chopped

500g (1lb 2oz) lean minced beef

35g (1¼oz) taco seasoning

150g (5½oz) uncooked quinoa, rinsed

1 red or orange pepper, deseeded and cut into bite-sized pieces

400g can chopped tomatoes

500ml (16fl oz) beef stock

1 tbsp tomato purée

400g can black beans, drained

salt and freshly ground black pepper

handful of coriander leaves, roughly chopped, to garnish

4–6 tbsp soured cream, to serve

1 Preheat the oven to 180°C (350°F/Gas 4). Heat the oil in a large ovenproof casserole over a medium heat. Add the onions and sauté for about 5 minutes, until translucent. Then add the beef and cook for about 5 minutes, stirring frequently, until browned. Add the taco seasoning, stir to mix, and cook for about 2 minutes.

2 Add the quinoa to the casserole and mix to combine. Then add the peppers, tomatoes, stock, and tomato purée. Mix well, cover, and place in the oven. Bake for about 30 minutes. Then remove from the oven, stir well to ensure the chilli is not sticking to the bottom, and return to the oven for a further 15 minutes.

3 Remove the casserole from the oven and add the beans. Mix to combine and return to the oven for a further 15 minutes or until the peppers are tender and the quinoa is cooked. Remove from the heat and season to taste. Garnish with coriander and serve hot with soured cream.

GRAIN EXCHANGE

For a variation, replace the quinoa with the same amount of **millet**.

why not try…

You could try replacing the black beans with the same quantity of **red kidney beans**.

RED LENTIL AND BULGUR WHEAT KORMA

In this vegan curry, korma paste is used for a light spiciness, along with coconut milk and bulgur wheat for a creamy texture.

SERVES 4 · PREP 5 MINS · COOK 40 MINS

1 tbsp coconut oil	500ml (16fl oz) vegetable stock
1 onion, finely chopped	
4 tbsp korma paste	200g (7oz) cauliflower, cut into florets
100g (3½oz) bulgur wheat	
100g (3½oz) red lentils	handful of coriander leaves, to garnish
400ml can coconut milk	

1 Heat the oil in a large saucepan over a medium heat. Add the onions and cook for 5 minutes, stirring frequently, until translucent. Then add the korma paste and cook, stirring constantly, for about 1 minute. Add the bulgur wheat, lentils, coconut milk, stock, and cauliflower. Mix well to combine.

2 Reduce the heat to a simmer and cook for about 30 minutes, stirring frequently, until the bulgur wheat is cooked, the cauliflower is tender, and the texture is thick and creamy. Remove from the heat, garnish with coriander, and serve hot.

CAJUN PRAWN AND SAUSAGE BAKE WITH FREEKEH

A twist on the traditional jambalaya, this dish uses freekeh in place of rice for a spicy yet wholesome and filling dinner.

SERVES 4 · PREP 5 MINS · COOK 50 MINS

225g (8oz) prawns, peeled and deveined	½ tbsp Cajun seasoning
1 andouille sausage, about 115g (4oz) in total, cut into 5mm (¼in) thin slices	400g can chopped tomatoes, with juices
	150g (5½oz) uncooked freekeh
225g (8oz) red potatoes, cut into 2.5cm (1in) pieces	salt and freshly ground black pepper

1 Preheat the oven to 200°C (400°F/Gas 6). Place the prawns, sausages, and potatoes in a 20 x 28cm (8 x 11in) baking dish. Spread them out in a single layer, sprinkle over the Cajun seasoning, and mix well. Top with the tomatoes and juices and bake in the oven for 40–50 minutes, stirring twice, until the potatoes are tender and cooked through.

2 Meanwhile, place the freekeh in a large, lidded saucepan and cover with 600ml (1 pint) of water. Bring to the boil, then reduce the heat to medium-low. Cover and cook for 20–25 minutes. Remove from the heat and drain any remaining water.

3 Transfer the freekeh to a large serving dish, add the prawn and sausage mixture, and stir well to combine. Season to taste with salt and pepper, if needed, and serve immediately.

BEEF CHiPOTLE CHiLLi

inspired by the original Texan chilli, this recipe mixes beef with millet for a hearty and filling meal. The chipotle chilli turns the sauce into a really spicy mixture, which can be countered with a dollop of cold soured cream.

SERVES 4 · PREP 30 MiNS · COOK 1 HR 10 MiNS

1–2 tbsp olive oil

450g (1lb) lean minced beef

450g (1lb) stewing beef pieces

1 onion

3 garlic cloves

1 chipotle chilli in adobo, plus 1 tsp sauce extra

500g can passata

400g can chopped tomatoes, with juices

170g can tomato purée

1 tbsp chilli powder

2 tsp cumin

50g (1¾oz) uncooked millet

salt and freshly ground black pepper

handful of coriander leaves, to garnish (optional)

1 Heat the oil in a Dutch oven or a large casserole over a medium heat. Add the minced and stewing beef and cook for about 5 minutes, stirring occasionally, until well browned. Drain any excess fat from the pan. Place the onion, garlic, and chipotle chilli and sauce in a food processor and pulse until the mixture is almost smooth. Add the mixture to the pot and stir to combine. Cook the mixture for a further 5 minutes, stirring frequently.

2 Add the passata, tomatoes and juices, tomato purée, chilli powder, and cumin. Add about 60ml (2fl oz) of water and stir well to mix. Then reduce the heat to a low simmer, cover, and cook for about 45 minutes. Check the chilli occasionally to make sure it does not stick to the pot and add more water if needed.

3 Meanwhile, rinse the millet under cold running water, drain, and place in a small saucepan. Cover with 170ml (6fl oz) of water and bring to the boil. Then reduce the heat to a medium-low, cover, and cook for about 15 minutes. Remove from the heat.

4 Add the millet, along with any remaining water, to the pot and stir well to ensure that it is evenly incorporated. Then cover and cook for a further 15–20 minutes. Remove from the heat, taste, and adjust the seasoning if needed. Serve hot, garnished with coriander, if using.

VEGETABLE DALIA STEW WITH BULGUR WHEAT

A "dalia" is a soft mix of vegetables and whole grains that is great for the digestion.

SERVES 6 · PREP 10 MINS · COOK 1 HR

1 tbsp light olive oil	200g (7oz) bulgur wheat
1 onion, finely chopped	150g (5½oz) red lentils
1½ tsp ground turmeric	1.5 litres (2¾ pints) vegetable stock
2 celery sticks, chopped into small pieces	salt and freshly ground black pepper
1 carrot, cut into small pieces	6 tbsp roughly chopped coriander leaves, to garnish
200g (7oz) potato, cut into 2cm (¾in) cubes	
150g (5½oz) cauliflower, cut into florets	

1 Heat the oil in a large soup pot over a medium heat. Add the onions and sauté for 5 minutes. Add the turmeric and cook, stirring frequently, for 1 minute. Then stir in the celery, carrots, potatoes, and cauliflower. Mix well and cook for 1 minute.

2 Add the bulgur wheat, lentils, and stock to the pot and mix well to combine. Reduce the heat to a simmer, cover, and cook for 50 minutes or until the vegetables are tender and the bulgur wheat is cooked. Season to taste, stir well, and remove from the heat. Garnish with coriander and serve hot.

SLOW COOKER BEEF AND VEGETABLE STEW

This warming, slow cooker dish is as easy to make as it is satisfying.

SERVES 6 · PREP 20 MINS · COOK 12 HRS

4 tbsp plain flour	6 garlic cloves, roasted, sliced, and crushed
salt and freshly ground black pepper	80g (2¾oz) uncooked kamut
550g (1¼lb) stewing beef, cut into 2.5cm (1in) chunks	1 litre (1¾ pints) beef stock
1 onion, diced	250ml (9fl oz) red wine
2 waxy potatoes, diced	
3 carrots, diced	

1 Place the flour in a shallow dish and season with salt and pepper. Add the beef and toss to coat. Place the beef, onions, potatoes, carrots, garlic, and kamut in a slow cooker and mix well.

2 Pour in the stock and wine, season to taste, and stir lightly to mix. Place the cooker on a low heat and cook for 10–12 hours. Then remove from the heat and serve hot. Store the leftovers in an airtight container in the fridge for up to five days.

AMARANTH AND WHITE BEAN CHILLI

This rich, creamy vegetarian chilli gets its heartiness from the amaranth, which works brilliantly as a thickener and combines well with the cannellini beans to give this dish an earthy flavour.

SERVES 4 · PREP 10 MINS · COOK 40 MINS

3 tbsp grapeseed oil

3 onions, diced

2 poblano chillies, deseeded and diced

6 garlic cloves, crushed

2 x 425g can cannellini beans

20g (¾oz) chopped coriander leaves, plus extra to garnish

1 tbsp oregano

¼ tsp cayenne pepper

½ tsp ground cumin

salt and freshly ground black pepper

750ml (1¼ pints) vegetable stock

250ml (9fl oz) whole milk

50g (1¾oz) uncooked amaranth

475g (1lb 1 oz) soured cream or plain Greek yogurt, plus extra to serve

1 Heat the oil in a large, heavy-based saucepan over a medium heat. Add the onions and poblano chillies and cook for about 5 minutes, stirring occasionally, until the onions are translucent. Then add the garlic and cook for a further 2 minutes.

2 Add the cannellini beans, coriander, oregano, cayenne pepper, and cumin to the pan. Season with ¼ teaspoon of salt, stir to mix, and cook for about 1 minute. Then add the stock, milk, and amaranth. Mix well and bring to the boil.

3 Reduce the heat to a simmer and cook for about 30 minutes or until it reduces and thickens. Add the soured cream and stir to combine. Remove from the heat and taste and adjust the seasoning, if needed. Serve warm, garnished with coriander.

onions

RED WiNE-BRAiSED BEETROOT AND LENTiLS WiTH FARRO

Beetroot and lentils are a match made in heaven when braised in a full-bodied red wine. Be sure to use a wine of good quality, as it will enhance the flavour of the stew and you can save a glass to have with your meal.

SERVES 4 · PREP 30 MiNS, PLUS OVERNiGHT SOAKiNG AND CHiLLiNG · COOK 1 HR 20 MiNS

150g (5½oz) uncooked farro

3 tbsp light olive oil

1 garlic clove, sliced

salt and freshly ground black pepper

250g (9oz) Greek yogurt

1 tbsp lemon juice

1 tsp lemon zest

1 small garlic clove, crushed

1 tbsp extra virgin olive oil

handful of flat-leaf parsley

FOR THE LENTiLS AND VEGETABLES

1 onion, finely sliced

3 garlic cloves, crushed

3 large beetroots, peeled and chopped into 3cm (1in) pieces

2 carrots, chopped into 2.5cm (1in) pieces

2 tsp tomato purée

100g (3½oz) black beluga lentils, rinsed and cleaned

200ml (7fl oz) good-quality red wine, such as a cabernet

250ml (9fl oz) vegetable stock

sprig each of rosemary and thyme

1 bay leaf

1 Place the farro in a large bowl, cover with water, and leave to soak overnight or for up to 12 hours. Then drain and rinse under running water. Drain well.

2 Heat 1 tablespoon of the light olive oil in a saucepan over a medium heat. Add the farro and sliced garlic. Season to taste with salt and cook for 5 minutes, stirring occasionally, until the farro is lightly toasted. Add 900ml (1½ pints) of water and bring to the boil. Then reduce the heat to a simmer, cover, and cook for 25–30 minutes or until the farro is tender. Drain any remaining water and rinse under running water. Drain well and set aside.

3 For the lentils and vegetables, heat the remaining light olive oil in a large, heavy-based, lidded saucepan over a medium heat. Add the onions and cook for 2–3 minutes or until softened. Then add the garlic, beetroot, and carrots. Season to taste with a good grinding of pepper and cook for 5–10 minutes, stirring occasionally. Add the tomato purée in a corner of the pan, cook for 1–2 minutes, then stir to mix with the vegetables.

4 Add the lentils, wine, stock, rosemary, thyme, and bay leaf. Bring to the boil. Then reduce the heat to a simmer and cook, covered, for 25 minutes or until the lentils and vegetables are cooked through. Season with salt and cook for a further 5–10 minutes. Remove from the heat and discard the rosemary, thyme, and bay leaf.

5 Place the yogurt, lemon juice, lemon zest, crushed garlic, and extra virgin olive oil in a bowl. Finely chop the parsley and add to the bowl. Season with a pinch of salt and whisk to combine. Cover with cling film and chill for 15 minutes. To serve, divide the farro between four serving plates, top with the beetroot and lentils, and spoon over a dollop of yogurt.

ALL THiNGS
SWEET

PUFFED SORGHUM SALTED CARAMEL POPCORN BALLS

This easy-to-make recipe uses sugar-free caramel, pecans, and popped sorghum to transform a popular snack into a delightful sweet and salty homemade treat that everyone will enjoy.

MAKES 12 BALLS · PREP 15 MiNS, PLUS COOLING · COOK 20 MiNS

100g (3½oz) uncooked sorghum

1 tbsp vegetable oil

75g (2½oz) corn kernels

100g (3½oz) pecans, roughly chopped

FOR THE CARAMEL

125ml (4¼fl oz) maple syrup

30g (1oz) unsalted butter

1 tsp cider vinegar

½ tsp salt

1 Heat a large, lidded saucepan over a medium heat for 5–10 minutes. Add half the sorghum to the pan and cover. Shake the pan lightly at regular intervals until the grain starts to pop. Remove the sorghum when the popping stops or slows to less than every 5 seconds. Repeat with the remaining sorghum. Place the popped grain in a large bowl and set aside to cool.

2 Increase the heat to medium-high and pour the oil into the pan. Once the oil is hot, add one-third of the corn kernels, cover, and shake the pan lightly to help them pop. Remove the popped corn and repeat with the remaining kernels. Remove from the heat and add to the popped sorghum. Leave to cool for 5 minutes. Then sift through to remove any hard kernels or sorghum grains. Add the pecans and mix well to combine.

3 For the caramel, heat a non-stick frying pan over a medium-high heat. Add the maple syrup, butter, cider vinegar, and 60ml (2fl oz) of water. Bring to the boil, then reduce to a rolling simmer. Cook for 10 minutes, stirring occasionally, until reduced to a thick and sticky caramel. Make sure the ingredients do not splash out of the pan as they will be hot.

4 Remove from the heat and leave to cool for about 2 minutes. Then add the salt and stir to mix. Pour over the sorghum, popcorn, and pecan mixture. Mix to coat and leave to cool. When cool enough to handle, form the mixture into 12 balls, pressing firmly to ensure that they stick. Place the balls on a baking sheet to cool and harden. Store in an airtight container.

STRAWBERRY POLENTA SHORTCAKES

These little "sandwiches" are a lovely adaptation of the traditional shortcake. They make excellent use of polenta to produce the perfect dessert for summer, when you can take advantage of a glut of strawberries.

SERVES 6 · PREP 30 MiNS · COOK 40 MiNS

200g (7oz) polenta

2 tbsp light olive oil

40g (1½oz) sugar

1 tsp vanilla extract

300ml (10fl oz) double cream

500g (1lb 2oz) strawberries

20g (¾oz) icing sugar

1 Preheat the oven to 190°C (375°F/Gas 5). Line two baking trays with greaseproof paper and set aside. Place 1 litre (1¾ pints) of water in a large saucepan and bring to a simmer. Then add the polenta and cook for 2–3 minutes, stirring constantly, until it has thickened. Remove from the heat and leave to cool for about 2 minutes.

2 Add the oil, sugar, and vanilla extract and mix well. Divide the mixture equally between the two baking trays, spreading it out to a 5mm (¼in) thick layer. Place the trays in the oven and bake for 30 minutes or until the polenta is spongy and slightly firm to the touch. It should easily pull away from the paper. Remove from the heat and leave to cool.

3 Place the cooled polenta on a clean work surface and use a cookie cutter to cut out twelve 8cm (3in) wide rounds. Place the double cream in a large bowl and whisk until it is thick and holds its shape. Place one-third of the strawberries in a bowl and crush with the back of a fork. Add half the icing sugar and mix well to combine. Cut the remaining strawberries into thin slices.

4 To assemble the shortcakes, lay one polenta round on each of six plates. Top them with 1 tablespoon of the whipped cream, 1 tablespoon of the strawberry and sugar mixture, and a few slices of strawberries. Place the remaining polenta rounds on top and gently pat them dry with kitchen paper. Dust with icing sugar and serve immediately.

GOAT'S CHEESECAKE WITH AN ALMOND AND AMARANTH CRUST

This decadent dessert is given a healthy twist with the addition of yogurt and a wholesome crust made from earthy amaranth and crunchy almonds. Easy to make, the hardest part is waiting for the cake to set before serving yourself a slice.

SERVES 8–12 · PREP 10 MINS, PLUS COOLING · COOK 55 MINS

600g (1lb 5oz) goat's cheese, softened

225g (8oz) cream cheese, softened

150g (5½oz) cane sugar

225g (8oz) plain, low-fat Greek yogurt

1½ tsp vanilla extract

4 eggs

FOR THE BASE

100g (3½oz) ground almonds

60g (2oz) amaranth flour

60g (2oz) tapioca starch

50g (1¾oz) icing sugar

½ tsp salt

115g (4oz) butter, melted

1 Preheat the oven to 180°C (350°F/Gas 4). Grease a 23cm (9in) springform cake tin. For the base, place all the ingredients in a bowl and mix to combine. Press the mixture into the bottom of the tin, making sure it is evenly covered. Set aside.

2 Place the goat's cheese, cream cheese, and sugar in a food processor and pulse to combine. Then add the yogurt and vanilla extract and pulse until just incorporated. Scrape down the sides of the bowl and stir well. Add the eggs, one at a time, and pulse until thoroughly blended. Pour the mixture over the base and transfer the tin to the oven.

3 Bake the cake for 25 minutes. Then rotate it by 180 degrees and bake for a further 20–30 minutes, until the top is wobbly but set. If it starts to brown too quickly, cover loosely with a sheet of foil. Remove from the heat. Leave the cake in the tin to cool down to room temperature. Gently remove from the tin and serve.

BAKED APPLES STUFFED WITH KAMUT AND RAISINS

Like the traditional baked apples, this recipe is both delicious and healthy, with the added bonus of wholegrain kamut that brings with it a chewy texture and a nutty flavour.

SERVES 4 · PREP 15 MINS, PLUS SOAKING AND COOLING · COOK 1 HR 30 MINS

60g (2oz) uncooked kamut

6 cooking apples,
  such as Bramley

80g (2¾oz) raisins

2 tsp ground cinnamon

4 tbsp honey

100g (3½oz) unsalted butter

1 Place the kamut in a bowl, cover with water, and leave to soak for about 8 hours or for up to 24 hours. Then drain, rinse under running water, and drain well again.

2 Place the kamut in a saucepan and cover with water. Bring to the boil, then reduce the heat to a simmer, and cook for 40–45 minutes. Remove from the heat, drain any remaining water, and leave to cool.

3 Preheat the oven to 160°C (320°F/ Gas 3). Remove the cores from the apples, keeping the bottom 1cm (½in) intact. Make the hole in the centre of each apple about 2.5cm (1in) wide. Place the apples in a large, deep-sided, ovenproof casserole.

4 Place the raisins, cinnamon, honey, and 60g (2oz) of the butter in a bowl and mix to combine. Then add the cooled kamut and mix until evenly combined. Stuff the apples with equal quantities of the mixture. Top with the remaining butter.

5 Bake in the oven for 45 minutes– 1 hour, until tender and easily pierced with a knife. Check every 15 minutes and spoon any melting butter on top of the kamut to keep it soft and to prevent it from becoming crisp. Remove from the heat and serve warm.

GRAIN EXCHANGE

For a variation, use the same amount of any of the following grains in place of the kamut.

wheat berries

spelt

farro

why not try...

Try using the same amount of chopped **dates** in place of the raisins. You could also try adding 30g (1oz) of finely chopped **walnuts**.

ROAST STONE FRUIT WITH MILLET CRUMBLE

The traditional crumble dessert gets a makeover, as roasting stone fruit brings out their natural sweetness with no need for added sugar, while the millet and almonds create a crisp, gluten-free crumble topping.

SERVES 4-6 · PREP 15 MINS, PLUS COOLING · COOK 1 HR

FOR THE FILLING

800g (1¾lb) mixed fruit, such as peaches, nectarines, and plums, stoned and roughly chopped

1 tbsp coconut oil, room temperature

FOR THE CRUMBLE TOPPING

85g (3oz) millet flakes

85g (3oz) ground almonds

50g (1¾oz) coconut oil, chilled and diced

60g (2oz) unrefined caster sugar

1 Preheat the oven to 200°C (400°F/Gas 6). For the filling, place the fruit in a roasting tray, drizzle over the oil, and toss to coat. Roast in the oven for 20–30 minutes, until tender but still holding their shape. Remove from the oven and leave to cool for at least 10 minutes.

2 For the crumble topping, place the millet flakes and almonds in a bowl and mix well to combine. Rub in the oil and mix well until the mixture resembles rough breadcrumbs. Add the sugar and gently mix to combine.

3 Place the cooled fruit mixture in a 20 x 25cm (8 x 10in) shallow baking dish and spread it out in an even layer. Sprinkle the topping evenly over the fruit. Place in the oven and bake for 20–30 minutes, until the topping is golden brown. Remove from the heat and serve warm.

GRAIN EXCHANGE

You could also use the same amount of **quinoa flakes** instead of the millet flakes.

why not try...

For an alternative, try using the same amount of **apples** and **blackberries** in place of the stone fruit.

CREAMY COCONUT BARLEY
WiTH STRAWBERRY CHiA JAM

Forget the typical rice pudding as this new, healthier version combines delicious coconut milk with the grainy goodness of barley, along with superfood chia seeds, making it a great vegan dessert.

SERVES 4 · PREP 10 MiNS, PLUS OVERNiGHT SOAKiNG AND CHiLLiNG · COOK 30 MiNS

250g (9oz) uncooked pearl barley

500ml (16fl oz) full-fat coconut milk, plus extra if needed

90ml (3fl oz) honey

FOR THE JAM

400g (14oz) strawberries, stalks removed

2 tbsp honey

45g (1½oz) chia seeds

1 Place the pearl barley in a bowl, cover with water, and leave to soak overnight or for up to 8 hours. Then drain, rinse under running water, and drain well again.

2 For the jam, place the strawberries in a large bowl and roughly mash with the back of a fork so that they release some juices but still retain some texture. Add the honey and chia seeds and mix well to combine. Chill in the fridge until thickened.

3 Place the barley, coconut milk, and honey in a large saucepan and bring to the boil. Then reduce the heat to a simmer and cook for 25–30 minutes or until the barley is tender, but still chewy, and the mixture has reached a thick porridge-like consistency. Check frequently and add more milk if the mixture seems too dry or if the liquid is absorbed too quickly. Remove from the heat. Divide the barley between four dishes. Top with 2–3 tablespoons of the jam and serve warm or at room temperature.

strawberries

CHOCOLATE AND AMARANTH PUDDiNG

Minty chocolate pudding and whipped cream make a decadent dessert that your family will love.

SERVES 4 · PREP 10 MiNS · COOK 30 MiNS

75g (2½oz) uncooked amaranth	350ml (12fl oz) milk
60g (2oz) granulated sugar	½ tsp mint extract
30g (1oz) unsweetened cocoa powder	120ml (4fl oz) double cream
2 tbsp cornflour	2 tbsp icing sugar
	½ tsp vanilla extract

1 Place 225ml (8fl oz) of water in a lidded, saucepan and bring to the boil. Add the amaranth, cover, and reduce the heat to medium-low. Cook for about 20 minutes or until all the water has been absorbed. Remove from the heat and set side.

2 Meanwhile, in a separate saucepan, place the sugar, cocoa powder, cornflour, and milk. Mix to combine and bring to the boil over a medium heat, stirring constantly. Then reduce the heat to low and cook for 2 minutes, until thickened. Remove from the heat, add the mint extract, and stir to combine.

3 Divide the pudding into two equal parts. Stir the amaranth into one half of the pudding, allow to cool slightly, and divide evenly between four tall glasses. Top each with the remaining half of the pudding.

4 Place the double cream, icing sugar, and vanilla extra in a bowl and use a hand-held blender to process until light and fluffy. Top each pudding with one-quarter of the cream and serve immediately.

SPiCED FRUiTY MiLLET CAKE

Just right for family and friends, this delicious cake will disappear in an instant.

SERVES 8–9 · PREP 10 MiNS · COOK 50 MiNUTES

125g (4½oz) couscous	1 large egg, beaten
100g (3½oz) uncooked millet	2 tsp ground cinnamon
100g (3½oz) raisins	1 tsp grated fresh root ginger
350ml (12fl oz) full-fat strawberry yogurt	

1 Place the couscous in a bowl and cover with 150ml (5fl oz) of boiling water. Cover with a plate and leave to sit.

2 Rinse the millet and place in a saucepan with 250ml (9fl oz) of water. Bring to the boil, then reduce the heat to a simmer. Cook for 15–20 minutes or until all the water has been absorbed and the millet is tender and fluffy. Remove from the heat and leave to cool.

3 Preheat the oven to 200°C (400°F/Gas 6). Grease and line a 23cm (9in) square baking dish with greaseproof paper. Add the couscous to the millet and fluff together with a fork, breaking up any lumps that have formed.

4 Add the raisins, yogurt, egg, and spices to the millet and couscous. Mix well to combine and transfer to the prepared dish. Smooth over the top and bake in the oven for 30 minutes, until it is firm to the touch and golden, and a skewer inserted into the centre comes out clean. Remove from the heat and serve warm.

SWEET SPICED FREEKEH
WITH FRESH FIGS

Inspired by the cuisine of the Middle East, in this dish the freekeh is cooked with sweet spices to enhance its flavour and served with honey, pistachios, and figs for an aromatic and mouth-watering dessert.

SERVES 4 · PREP 5 MINS · COOK 25 MINS

100g (3½oz) cracked freekeh

1 star anise

4 cardamom pods

1 tsp ground cinnamon

½ tsp grated fresh root ginger

¼ tsp grated nutmeg

¼ tsp salt

8 fresh figs, stems removed

4 tbsp honey, plus extra
   to serve

40g (1½oz) pistachios,
   roughly chopped

2 tbsp chopped mint leaves

4 tbsp Greek yogurt, to serve

1 Place the freekeh, star anise, cardamom, cinnamon, ginger, and nutmeg in a large saucepan. Add the salt and cover with 500ml (16fl oz) of water. Place the pan over a medium heat and bring to the boil. Then reduce the heat to a simmer and cook for about 15 minutes or until all the liquid has been absorbed.

2 Meanwhile, preheat the grill to its medium setting. Grease and line a baking tray with greaseproof paper. Cut a cross in the top of each fig, cutting almost to the bottom so they open up like a flower. Place on the baking sheet and drizzle with 2 tablespoons of honey. Place the tray under the grill and cook for 10 minutes or until the figs are lightly grilled.

3 Remove and discard the star anise and cardamom pods. Add the remaining honey to the cooked freekeh and mix well. Divide the freekeh mixture between four plates. Top each plate with two grilled figs and a quarter of the pistachios. Garnish with mint and drizzle with honey, if you wish. Serve with Greek yogurt.

GRAIN EXCHANGE

In place of the freekeh, use the same quantity of either of the following grains.

teff

polenta

CHOCOLATE, HAZELNUT, AND BUCKWHEAT CAKE

Buckwheat flour naturally complements the creamy chocolate and subtle hazelnut and vanilla flavouring in this decadent cake. Serve it as it is, or with a scoop of vanilla ice cream for the perfect after dinner indulgence.

MAKES 1 · PREP 30 MiNS · COOK 35 MiNS

100g (3½oz) butter, melted, plus extra for greasing

60g (2oz) hazelnuts

100g (3½oz) dark chocolate, at least 70 per cent cocoa solids, broken into pieces

4 large eggs, lightly beaten

100g (3½oz) coconut palm sugar or light brown sugar

¼ tsp sea salt

1 tsp vanilla extract

35g (1¼oz) buckwheat flour

1 Preheat the oven to 180°C (350°F/Gas 4). Grease and line a 23cm (9in) cake tin with parchment paper. Place the hazelnuts on a baking sheet and roast in the oven for about 5 minutes, or until they are lightly browned and the skins have loosened. Remove from the heat and leave to cool.

2 Once cool enough to handle, lightly rub the hazelnuts between your hands, or a kitchen towel, to remove the skins. Place them in a food processor and pulse until reduced to a coarse flour. Remove from the food processor and set aside.

3 Place the chocolate in a bowl and set over a pan of simmering water to melt. Place the eggs, sugar, and salt in a bowl and whisk until the mixture doubles in size. Then gently fold in the vanilla extract, butter, and melted chocolate. Add the hazelnut flour and buckwheat flour and gently fold the batter to incorporate all the ingredients.

4 Spoon the batter into the cake tin, in a smooth and even layer. Bake for about 30 minutes or until a skewer inserted into the centre comes out clean. Remove from the heat and leave to cool in the tin. Then transfer the cake to a serving platter and serve at room temperature.

LAVENDER AND LEMON BARS WITH A SPELT CRUST

A slight twist on the classic lemon bars, this recipe uses lavender, tapioca, and spelt flour in the crust to add a floral and earthy note to this heavenly dessert.

MAKES 18 · PREP 15 MINS, PLUS CHILLING · COOK 40 MINS

FOR THE CRUST

150g (5½oz) spelt flour

40g (1½oz) tapioca starch

50g (1¾oz) icing sugar

½ tsp salt

1 tbsp finely chopped lavender

1 tsp grated lemon zest

115g (4oz) butter, chilled and diced, plus extra for greasing

FOR THE FILLING

225g (8oz) caster sugar

4 eggs

120ml (4fl oz) lemon juice

50g (1¾oz) spelt flour

¼ tsp salt

1 tsp vanilla extract

2 tbsp icing sugar, for dusting

1 Preheat the oven to 180°C (350°F/Gas 4). Grease a 20 x 28cm (8 x 11in) baking tin. For the crust, place the flour, starch, sugar, salt, lavender, and lemon zest in a large bowl and mix well. Then add the butter and rub it in until the mixture resembles coarse breadcrumbs.

2 Transfer the mixture to the baking tin and spread it out in an even layer. Place the tin in the oven and bake for about 20 minutes or until lightly browned. Remove from the heat and set aside. Reduce the oven temperature to 160°C (325°F/Gas 3).

3 Meanwhile, for the filling, place the sugar and eggs in a bowl and cream together using a hand-held blender, until it turns a pale yellow. Then add the lemon juice, flour, salt, and vanilla extract to the bowl. Beat the ingredients until well combined.

4 Pour the custard mixture over the crust and bake for a further 20 minutes or until the filling has set. Remove from the heat and leave to cool, until it reaches room temperature. Then transfer to an airtight container and chill in the fridge for at least 1 hour. Serve chilled dusted with icing sugar.

ALMOND POLENTA CAKE
WITH RASPBERRIES

This gluten-free cake is perfect for satisfying your sweet tooth while staying away from flour. The polenta and almonds give the cake a crumbly texture that beautifully offsets the tartness of the raspberries.

SERVES 8-10 · PREP 15 MINS, PLUS COOLING · COOK 45 MINS

200g (7oz) unsalted butter

230g (8oz) unrefined
  caster sugar

3 large eggs

1 tsp almond extract

200g (7oz) ground almonds

100g (3½oz) polenta

1½ tsp baking powder

200g (7oz) raspberries

20g (¾oz) flaked almonds

1 Preheat the oven to 180°C (350°F/Gas 4). Grease and line a 23cm (9in) springform cake tin with greaseproof paper. Cream the butter and sugar with an electric whisk for 2 minutes or until light and fluffy. Add the eggs one at a time, mixing well between additions. Then add the almond extract and whisk for 2 minutes until fully incorporated.

2 Place the ground almonds, polenta, and baking powder in a separate bowl and mix well. Lightly fold the dry mixture into the butter, sugar, and egg mixture until just smooth. Gently fold the raspberries into the batter. Spoon the batter into the prepared tin, smooth over the surface, and scatter over the flaked almonds.

3 Bake the cake for 45 minutes or until golden brown and a skewer inserted into the centre comes out with only a few crumbs. Leave the cake in the tin to cool slightly. Then transfer to a wire rack to cool completely before serving. Store in the fridge, in an airtight container, for up to 3 days.

LEMON AND BLUEBERRY BULGUR WHEAT BAKE

The lemon and blueberries create a tangy duo in this delightfully light and creamy bake that uses bulgur wheat as its base. It's perfect for a lunch party as an alternative to summer pudding.

SERVES 6–8 · PREP 10 MINS · COOK 1 HR 15 MINUTES

200g (7oz) bulgur wheat

1 tbsp unsalted butter

2 large eggs

120ml (4fl oz) milk

grated zest of 3 lemons

85g (3oz) unrefined caster sugar

200g (7oz) blueberries

1 Place the bulgur wheat in a large saucepan and cover with 500ml (16fl oz) of water. Bring to the boil, then reduce the heat to a simmer, and cover. Cook for about 15 minutes or until all the water is absorbed and the bulgur wheat is tender. Remove from the heat and set aside to cool.

2 Preheat the oven to 180°C (350°F/Gas 4). Grease a 1.5 litre (2¾ pint) ovenproof dish and set aside. Place the eggs and milk in a bowl. Whisk to combine, then add the lemon zest, and whisk again until well incorporated.

3 Place the bulgur wheat in a separate large bowl. Add the sugar and blueberries and mix well. Then add the egg and milk mixture and mix until well incorporated. Transfer the mixture to the prepared dish and bake for 1 hour, until golden on top and just set in the middle. Serve warm, with cream or yogurt.

GRAIN EXCHANGE

You could replace the bulgur wheat with the same amount of **freekeh**.

why not try...

Instead of blueberries, you could use the same amount of **raspberries**.

SPELT AND OLIVE OIL CAKE

This filling cake is flavoured by the unique combination of olive oil and blood orange juice. You could also use a different, or seasonal, citrus fruit, such as Meyer lemons, for the same result.

SERVES 12 · PREP 10 MINS, PLUS COOLING AND SETTING · COOK 40 MINS

120ml (4fl oz) extra virgin olive oil, plus extra for greasing

225g (8oz) spelt flour

100g (3½oz) ground almonds

grated zest of 1 blood orange

2 tsp baking powder

1 tsp salt

125ml (4fl oz) blood orange juice

2 eggs

150g (5½oz) light brown sugar

FOR THE GLAZE

1 tsp blood orange juice

35g (1oz) icing sugar

1 Preheat the oven to 180°C (350°F/Gas 4). Grease and line a 23cm (9in) round cake tin with baking parchment. Place the spelt flour, ground almonds, blood orange zest, baking powder, and salt in a bowl and mix well until combined.

2 Place the oil, blood orange juice, eggs, and sugar in a separate bowl. Whisk to combine. Make a well in the centre of the dry ingredients and pour in the oil mixture. Mix until just incorporated, making sure you don't over-mix the batter.

3 Transfer the mixture to the prepared cake tin. Bake for 35–40 minutes or until the top of the cake is golden brown and a skewer inserted into the centre comes out clean. Remove from the heat and leave to rest for about 10 minutes. Then carefully flip the cake out of the tin and transfer to a wire rack to cool slightly.

4 Meanwhile, for the glaze, place the blood orange juice, icing sugar, and 2 teaspoons of water in a bowl and whisk to combine. Pour the glaze over the cake and leave to set. Serve warm.

CHOCOLATE CHIP, PEANUT, AND BUCKWHEAT COOKIES

Gluten-free buckwheat flour adds to the nuttiness of these delicious cookies. Perfect for children and adults alike, enjoy them with a glass of milk or even your afternoon coffee!

MAKES 12 LARGE COOKIES · PREP 30 MINUTES, PLUS CHILLING AND COOLING · COOK 15 MINUTES

110g (4oz) unsalted butter

175g (6oz) brown sugar

1 large egg

200g (7oz) buckwheat flour

¼ tsp salt

½ tsp baking powder

85g (3oz) dark chocolate chips

85g (3oz) salted peanuts

1 Line two baking sheets with greaseproof paper and set aside. In a large bowl, cream together the butter and sugar with an electric whisk until light and fluffy. Then beat the egg into the mixture until well combined.

2 Place the flour, salt, and baking powder in a separate bowl and mix well. Fold the dry mixture into the butter, sugar, and egg mixture, a little at a time, until thoroughly incorporated. Add the chocolate chips and peanuts to the mixture and stir well to incorporate. Cover the dough with cling film and chill in the fridge for about 30 minutes. Preheat the oven to 180°C (350°F/Gas 4).

3 Place golf ball-sized pieces of the dough on the prepared baking sheets and flatten them gently. Make sure they are placed at least 5cm (2in) apart, as they will spread while baking. Bake the cookies for about 15 minutes, until they start to turn golden but still look a little under baked. Remove from the heat and leave on the baking sheet for at least 10 minutes to cool and firm up. Then transfer to a wire rack to cool completely. Store in an airtight container.

GRILLED PEACHES WITH ICE CREAM AND WHOLEGRAIN GRANOLA

Grilled peaches are one of summer's tastiest treats. Paired here with a healthy amaranth and millet granola, they are easy to prepare and can also be stored overnight for a filling wholegrain breakfast.

SERVES 4 · PREP 10 MINS · COOK 20 MINS

4 peaches, pitted and halved

2 tbsp grapeseed oil

4 scoops of vanilla ice cream

FOR THE GRANOLA

100g (3½oz) rolled oats

50g (1¾oz) uncooked amaranth

50g (1¾oz) uncooked millet

75g (2½oz) almonds, chopped

40g (1½oz) pumpkin seeds

1 tbsp virgin coconut oil

2 tbsp maple syrup (grade B)

½ tsp vanilla extract

¼ tsp ground cinnamon

¼ tsp sea salt

1 Preheat the oven to 180°C (350°F/Gas 4). For the granola, place all the ingredients in a large bowl and toss to combine. Spread the mixture evenly in a baking tray and place in the oven. Bake the granola for 10–15 minutes or until the oats and nuts are lightly browned. Remove from the heat and leave to cool.

2 Meanwhile, set the grill at its medium setting. Brush the peach skins with the oil and place under the grill for 2–3 minutes, on each side, until tender. Remove from the heat. Place the grilled peaches in serving dishes, then top with a scoop of vanilla ice cream and the granola. Serve immediately.

STRAWBERRY AND PEACH GALETTE WITH WHEAT BERRIES

Literally meaning a flat crusty cake, a galette is perfectly accompanied by summer fruit such as strawberries and peaches. The wheat berries in this recipe give the pastry a fresh taste and a hearty, crunchy texture.

SERVES 6 · PREP 25 MINS, PLUS CHILLING AND SOAKING · COOK 40–45 MINS

200g (7oz) soft wheat berries

1 tbsp caster sugar

¼ tsp salt

115g (4oz) unsalted butter, chilled and diced

FOR THE FILLING

2 ripe peaches, stoned and sliced

300g (10oz) strawberries, trimmed and halved

2 tbsp honey

½ tsp orange juice or lemon juice

1 tsp vanilla extract

1 Place the wheat berries in a coffee grinder and grind into a fine flour. Sift the flour into a bowl, removing any remaining hard pieces. Transfer 180g (6½oz) of the flour to a large bowl, reserving the remaining flour for dusting. Add the sugar and salt to the flour and mix well. Rub in the butter and combine until the mixture resembles rough breadcrumbs.

2 Add 3–4 tablespoons of chilled water, a little at a time, and combine with the flour mixture until it forms a dough. Form the dough into a ball and lightly press into a disc-like shape. Cover the dough with cling film and chill in the fridge for 30 minutes.

3 Meanwhile, for the filling, place all the ingredients in a large bowl and mix well. Leave for about 20 minutes, to draw the water out. Preheat the oven to 180°C (350°F/Gas 4) and line a baking sheet with baking parchment.

4 On a lightly floured surface, roll out the pastry to a 25cm (10in) circle.
If the pastry is too hard, allow it to reach room temperature and soften before rolling it out. Drain and discard the liquid from the fruit mixture. Place the fruit in the centre of the pastry circle. Then fold up the pastry to enclose the fruit, and crimp the edges with your fingers to decorate.

5 Bake in the oven for 40–45 minutes or until the crust is golden brown and the fruit is bubbling. Remove from the oven and leave to cool slightly. Serve warm.

WHOLE GRAIN CHOCOLATE CHIP PIE

This pie version of your favourite chocolate chip cookie is also full of wholesome goodness and is best served warm with a big scoop of vanilla ice-cream for a delicious treat.

SERVES 6 · PREP 20 MINUTES, PLUS COOLING AND CHILLING · COOK 1 HR 30 MINS

50g (1¾oz) uncooked amaranth

2 large eggs

75g (2½oz) wholewheat flour

½ tsp salt

100g (3½oz) granulated sugar

100g (3½oz) brown sugar

175g (6oz) butter, softened

1 tbsp vanilla extract

300g (10oz) chocolate chips

icing sugar, for dusting

FOR THE BISCUIT CASE

175g (6oz) digestive biscuits

60g (2oz) demerara sugar

85g (3oz) butter, melted

1 Preheat the oven to 180°C (350°F/Gas 4). For the biscuit case, crush the biscuits by hand or pulse in a food processor until they resemble fine breadcrumbs. Place the crumbs in a large bowl and add the sugar and butter. Mix until the mixture resembles wet sand.

2 Spoon the mixture into a 23cm (9in) loose-bottomed tart tin. Press the mixture firmly into the bottom and sides of the tin, making sure it is as packed as possible and there is a good side to the case. Place the case on a baking sheet and bake for about 10 minutes. Remove from the heat and set aside to cool before chilling for at least 30 minutes.

3 Meanwhile, place the amaranth in a small saucepan and cover with 200ml (7fl oz) of water. Bring to a simmer and cook for about 40 minutes or until all the water has been absorbed. Drain any remaining water and rinse under running water. Set aside.

4 Place the eggs in a large bowl and process with a hand-held blender for about 3 minutes or until foamy. Add the flour, salt, and both lots of sugar. Beat the mixture until just combined. Then add the butter and vanilla extract and beat until well incorporated.

5 Add the amaranth and chocolate chips to the bowl and mix until evenly combined. Spoon the mixture into the biscuit case and spread into one even layer. Bake in the oven for 40 minutes, until a skewer inserted into it comes out clean. Transfer to a wire rack to cool. Dust with icing sugar and serve warm.

iNDEX

Entries in **bold** indicate ingredients.

ACKNOWLEDGMENTS

ABOUT THE AUTHORS

LAURA AGAR WiLSON is a health coach, writer, recipe developer, and author of the popular healthy living and lifestyle blog *wholeheartedlyhealthy.com*, where she shares healthy living tips and tricks, recipes, and her own personal healthy living journey. Her work has featured on *BBC Good Food*, *Grazia Daily*, and *Channel 4 Food* websites. She also writes regularly for the *Huffington Post* and has appeared in *Healthy Magazine* as a Healthy Hero.

JODi MORENO is a chef and food photographer who runs the food blog, *What's Cooking Good Looking*. Her work has been featured on countless sites, such as the *Huffington Post*, *Edible Magazine*, *Food52*, *Gourmet*, *Self Magazine*, *Buzzfeed*, *The Kitchn*, and *VegNews Magazine*. She was named by *Better Homes and Gardens* and *Shape Magazine* as one of the best healthy food bloggers, and *Saveur Magazine* selected her blog as one of the best overall blogs of 2014.

SARAH W. CARON is the senior features editor for the *Bangor Daily News* and a freelance writer, editor, and recipe developer. In addition to her newspaper column, Maine Course, she's written for publications including *Bella*, *Connecticut Magazine*, *Betty Crocker*, and *iVillage*. She also writes the food blog *sarahscucinabella.com*, which was voted one of the Top 25 foodie blogs by *FriendsEat* in 2009 and named as one of the "Sites We Love" by *Saveur Magazine*.

THANKS

Laura Agar Wilson would like to thank the team at DK "for involving me in this project and supporting me throughout"; her husband, James, for putting up with a very hectic and messy kitchen, and her best friend, Claire, for her support and feedback on recipes.

Jodi Moreno would like to thank her husband, Michael Moreno, for his endless support and washing of dishes.

DK would like to thank the following:
Photography: Charlotte Tolhurst for new recipe photography, and Jodi Moreno for the recipe photography on pages 32–33, 36–37, 62–63, 76–77, 118–119, 122–123, 126–127, 170–171, 180–181, 185, 192, 200–201, 208–209, 212–213, 230, and 239.
Photography art direction: Sara Robin, Geoff Fennell.
Food styling: Kate Wesson.
Prop styling: Rob Merrett.
Additonal image retouching: Adam Brackenberry, Tom Morse.
Technical support: Sonia Charbonnier.
Recipe testing: Laura Camerer Cuss, Katy Greenwood, and Jill Weatherburn.
Additional editorial work: Jill Weatherburn.
Proofreading: Katie Golsby, Dorothy Kikon, Janashree Singha, and Manasvi Vohra.
Indexing: Vanessa Bird.

All photography and artworks © Dorling Kindersley